T0339510

Temporal Politics and Banal Culture

This book addresses the absence of a strong alignment with the future in contemporary social life and explores anomalous temporal experience as a way to expand political imaginations. In the aftermath of the modern myth of progress, it argues we have entered into a kind of dystopia—brutal or seemingly benign—of the continual present that is resistant to systemic change but is nevertheless animated through cycles of novelty and obsolescence. Exploring a condition in which we are out of ideas and facing a 'non-future' of blind technical improvement and fear, the author examines the heterochronia of eerie atmospheres and temporal suspensions. Rather than a reinstatement of the great dream of The Future, a temporality of possibility is explored in strange dimensions of otherwise mundane sites: logistic spaces and ex-urban landscapes; boredom connected to digital media; and the material culture of a recently abandoned town. Drawing on contemporary social and cultural theory, as well as urban geography and media studies, the book develops its conceptual position through a series of vignettes of key sites and experiences. Through an elliptical and generative approach, it analyses zones where novelty collapses and where figures of defiance and possibility might emerge. A rigorous theoretical examination of contemporary life and culture grounded in a close examination of sites and material examples, *Temporal Politics and Banal Culture: Before the Future* will appeal to scholars of social theory, sociology, cultural geography, cultural studies and social philosophy.

Peter Conlin is a writer and researcher based in Birmingham, UK. He is a Teaching Associate at the University of Nottingham, has completed postdoctoral research at the Institute of European and American Studies, Academia Sinica, Taiwan, and is a co-facilitator of the Boredom Network research group. He is currently developing the Time Lapse podcast which is an interview series with theorists, activists and artists on temporal politics of the twenty-first century.

Classical and Contemporary Social Theory
Series Editor
Stjepan G. Mestrovic
Texas A&M University, USA

Classical and Contemporary Social Theory publishes rigorous scholarly work that re-discovers the relevance of social theory for contemporary times, demonstrating the enduring importance of theory for modern social issues. The series covers social theory in a broad sense, inviting contributions on both 'classical' and modern theory, thus encompassing sociology, without being confined to a single discipline. As such, work from across the social sciences is welcome, provided that volumes address the social context of particular issues, subjects, or figures and offer new understandings of social reality and the contribution of a theorist or school to our understanding of it.

The series considers significant new appraisals of established thinkers or schools, comparative works or contributions that discuss a particular social issue or phenomenon in relation to the work of specific theorists or theoretical approaches. Contributions are welcome that assess broad strands of thought within certain schools or across the work of a number of thinkers, but always with an eye toward contributing to contemporary understandings of social issues and contexts.

Titles in this series

Temporal Politics and Banal Culture
Before the Future
Peter Conlin

Revisiting Modernity and the Holocaust
Heritage, Dilemmas, Extensions
Edited by Jack Palmer and Dariusz Brzeziński

For more information about this series, please visit: www.routledge.com/sociology/series/ASHSER1383

Temporal Politics and Banal Culture

Before the Future

Peter Conlin

LONDON AND NEW YORK

First published 2022
by Routledge
4 Park Square, Milton Park, Abingdon, Oxon OX14 4RN

and by Routledge
605 Third Avenue, New York, NY 10158

Routledge is an imprint of the Taylor & Francis Group, an informa business

British Library Cataloguing-in-Publication Data
A catalogue record for this book is available from the British Library

Library of Congress Cataloging-in-Publication Data
A catalog record for this book has been requested

ISBN: 978-1-472-47437-7 (hbk)
ISBN: 978-1-032-24545-4 (pbk)
ISBN: 978-1-315-54894-4 (ebk)

DOI: 10.4324/9781315548944

Typeset in Times New Roman
by Apex CoVantage, LLC

Contents

Acknowledgements

David Graeber was right when he said that we should thank everyone we have ever met, because who knows where good ideas really come from. So I thank everyone I have ever had interesting encounters with and especially acknowledge David's irrepressible spirit. Thanks to Tina Kendall, Sam Gillies, Yann van der Cruyssen and Andy Goffey for the encouragement and feedback. Thanks also to the 16 Beaver assemblies for the inspiration and learning space. This book would not have been possible without Kirsten Forkert's continual faith and support.

To the memory of Murdy Daniel Conlin, whose spirit of invention and unconventional thinking opened a door.

Introduction

Part I: Concept, themes, ploys

> . . . [P]reparing to embark on incalculable journeys into the interior of time, to encounter there rhythms from which the sick shall draw strength as they did earlier on high mountains or on the shores of southern seas.
>
> (Benjamin 2000, 487)

> To look at what you wouldn't look at, to hear what you wouldn't listen to, to be attentive to the banal, to the ordinary, to the infra-ordinary. To deny the ideal hierarchy of the crucial and the incidental, because *there is no incidental*, only dominant cultures that exile us from ourselves and others, a loss of meaning which is for us not only a siesta of consciousness but also a decline in existence.
>
> (Virilio 2009, 47)

> [T]he future is the sign outside the No Future night club.
>
> (Bloch 1996, 5)

The starting point for this book is the assessment that the future, as a driving force for progressive movements and political imaginations in the West, has been dramatically weakened; but rather than a resurrection of the future, I will be exploring other temporal realms to rouse political imaginations. Despite all the zeal for the future primarily associated with the myth of technological advancement that is built into modern capitalism (trips to Mars, AI transformations, the coming of the singularity, etc.), a more generalised sense of a better future—beyond one's personal circumstances— is almost non-existent. An orientation to the future as a space of potential where different kinds of social transformation can occur is insubstantial in this conjuncture, and in so many urgent matters (climate change, socio-economic inequalities, mounting geopolitical tensions) the future is almost

DOI: 10.4324/9781315548944-1

synonymous with calamity. Are there ways of reinvigorating futural imaginations? Can we, or even if it was possible, should we resume the ideology of the progressive future? I do not see it as either possible or desirable
to re-enter the grand mythology of the modern future; instead, we should
move from 'The Future' to futurity and into sites and practices of temporal
possibilities. The ideas explored in this book are based on the supposition
that what is needed is not the future per se, but futural preconditions; and in
the attempt to circumvent impasses and conceptual exhaustion, I delve into
unusual sites and strange temporal modes. In particular, this investigation of
futural antecedents is based in sites of low-density culture—banality, types
of inactivity and outmodedness.

To introduce this further, the twentieth century is usually seen as an
overtly or even overly futuristic time, yet in the early twenty-first century,
the future itself appears vexing, uncertain and usually dystopian. Yet this is
in not really a simple dichotomy between the future and its absence, as the
aforementioned quotation by Ernst Bloch implies, certain forms of futurity often carry their own dissolution. In the West, and in many ways globally, the twentieth century was manifestly future-oriented in all its violence
and optimism for radical social transformation, progress imaginaries, the
maelstrom of modern life (Berman 2009), utopian projects and conquests—
the mass utopias (Buck-Morss 2002) of overcoming material scarcity, the
power of the atom, space travel, futuristic urbanism (in very different ways
Ebenezer Howard and Le Corbusier or Constant Nieuwenhuys' Situationist
city), and the futurism of various artistic movements (Constructivists, Futur-
ists, Surrealists and so on). Yet twenty-first-century futurism, if I can be
permitted such a generalisation as a way into a set of concepts and compli-
cations, seems harder to conceive owing to both an emergent proliferation
of different kinds of futures, and at the same time, difficult to imagine given
a collapse of the future as an orientation to a qualitatively different realm
(see Berardi 2011; Fisher 2014; Nowotny 2005). It would be a mistake to
say there is a total absence of thinking of the future in contemporary society
yet most of these conceptualisations remain just that—ideas of futurity that
lack larger social and political traction. Twenty-first-century social imaginations contain an impressive plurality of futures, yet these are generally either
grandiose presumptions or marginalised projects—the coming of 'the singularity,' the potentials of automation with a residual adherence to technocratic
'progress' yet with diminished claims of universal benefit, accelerationists
of both the left and the right, and the rise of non-Eurocentric futurism such
as indigenous futures or developments in Afrofuturism. Hence there is a
diversity of incipient and contradictory futures, at the same time as there
is a generalised condition of living 'after the future' (Berardi 2011); that is,
after the future as a collective project which holds an alterity and promise

beyond the oppressive practices of the present. In its place appear mounting reactionary movements, growing socio-economic inequality and paralysis in the face of the human-made climate crisis.

While largely accepting the diagnosis of a 'cancellation of the future' position, propounded in Franco Berardi's *After the Future* (2011) and Mark Fisher's writing (2013, 2014 and 2018), which I will discuss more extensively in Part II of this introduction, this book does not look for a reinstatement of the future, but rather, to strange time modes as a pre-futural force. This involves a political horizon emerging from counter-temporalisations within eerie atmospheres, from the encounter of lapses, gaps and suspensions, particularly related to the imbrication of novelty into obsolescence. In so doing, the book is a mediation on the politics of time in the early twenty-first century developed through an entanglement of spaces, media objects, material culture and landscapes. It is comprised of three main chapters which explore interconnections between mundane situations and space-time crystallisations which stir certain quadrants of the imagination: logistics (distribution centres on the edges of cities), boredom (as affective waste within cycles of novelty and outmodedness) and obsolescence (an exploration of the enigmatic town of Kitsault which was deserted shortly after its construction in the late 1970s and yet has been maintained; thus it is suspended from either falling into decay or becoming a lived community). A dimension in all of this—a grey tone sounding continually—is low-density culture. From the grand frontier of the future with its space ships and crystal cities, we move into the eerie time of the mundane, the nondescript, quotidian blandness and detritus. One can more likely associate alternate temporalities in extreme conditions—ecstatic states, rebellions, trauma, deserts and glaciers—yet the book follows a fascination for an invisible, enigmatic quality in ubiquity, in the unlikely itself. As if there is a latent charge in almost everything surrounding us, everything that is, which appears of little consequence; and under certain conditions, this could be activated and eradicate a deadening force within what is seen as the present. Yet in the meantime, in the general milieu, appear the quintessential scenes where nothing seems to happen. This is not a prelude to the final days when the last shall become first, rather speculation on subversion within the incidental itself—the profound middle consequence of the hitherto inconsequential.

As I will examine in more depth further on, I have come to the conclusion that it is better to let go of the future as the prime axis of political transformation and as the plane for thinking of collective possibility—letting go of the future, that is, in its name. Due to problematic legacies, all matter of impasses and depletions, it is more productive and captivating to explore temporality and possibility outside the rubric of the future as such. When we speak of the loss of futurity or the cancelation of the future, what is really addressed is the dominance of the continual present. If the essence of what is meant by futurity lies in unseating the temporal containment of the present, then that is the zone to explore whether it is identified as the future or not. Numerous theorists have laid out the case of a historical paralysis of the continual present including Paul Virilio, a through line in the work of Frederic Jameson, Helga Nowotny's sociological overview and is a key to Ernst Bloch's thought, in which we are confined in a here and now cut off from temporalities of possibility ('the darkness of the lived moment' (1996, 12)). What matters is the breaching of this temporal enclosure, not a resumption of 'the future' per se; and I see this occurring through an activation of more complex and often indefinite temporal relations referred to as heterochronic. We are caught in a present without a view, with weak connections to the past or the future. There is a contradiction, hopefully a productive one, that the crux of this book is a refusal of the dominance of the here and now, yet it works through banality—the very seat of the continual present—as its starting point.

As should be clear already, the ideas explored in this book are not within the metaphor of the future's glowing horizon, but in oblique glimmers and sideways apparitions. All along, we kept looking ahead—yearning, peering, but these collective hallucinations were in the wrong direction. It is side by side the present, if not closer still. No wonder they thought we were past it. An appositional dynamic like the multiverse replaces time travel in the political imagination—a different time, but beside us, not where the future was thought to be. The book is first and foremost about breaking the enchantment of the continual present and its aesthetico-political correlate of an irrepressible realism in which nothing ever seems possible other than what already exists, including prescriptions of the future itself. A vibrant imagination of what is to come is most of all based on temporal alterity, and I will be exploring this primarily in the anomalous fluctuations of banal sites however fleeting or otherwise bleak.

Modes of investigation

McKenzie Wark has written about a profound recomposition of critical theory in the time of the Anthropocene intersecting with the intensification of commodification. In the entwining of cultural and natural forces, and what ought to be a mind-bending confrontation with constraints coupled with the extension of temporal scales and the need for new forms of understanding, we are emerging out of a pre-history. 'Disparate times call for disparate methods. Let's just say that this is the end of pre-history, this moment when planetary constraints start really coming to bear on the ever-expanding universe of the commodification of everything' (Wark 2015, xi). My opening to this begins by working through conceptual knots and vignettes, and moving with currents of fascination as much as possible rather than being 'about them'. Embracing the need for disparate approaches, the writing in this book is elliptical and generative. While diminishing a more systemic understanding, it is attuned to sociopolitical atmospheres. It is also based on a view of contemporary life as bound within capitalist realism. This is Mark Fisher's (2009) term for the condition that despite such tumultuous circumstances, we are bound to the rationale that there is no other way for society to function than the existing capitalist formation, that human desire and social life itself has no other viable form than that which is organised through the personal accumulation of wealth. Because this term was coined in the first decade of the twenty-first century (pre-pandemic, before Trump, within the aftermath of third way neoliberalism of New Labour, still in the early onset of networked digital media, etc.), some readers might ask if we are still within this particular sense of inevitability. I will bracket off a more extensive argument for its continued relevance by pointing out the capitalist realism of the supposedly implacable logic of carbon offsetting and green capitalism (there can be no other way of responding to anthropogenic climate change); Elon Musk's dire realism of private techno 'solutions' while asserting the need to colonise other worlds because there can be no other way to live on the Earth that doesn't sooner or later destroy it; and the return of the capitalist real in post-pandemic austerity and data reductionism.

This 'realism' is inculcated in the atmospheres which we move, think and live through; and because of this environmental condition, presets possibilities and forecloses actions even before they can begin. Because of this, exploring atmospheres and in particular their anomalies is an essential focus of this book and the modes of investigation deployed herein. Following on from this, what I offer is often about seeing what is not supposed to be in the present, seeing around the edges of the ostensible, into overlaps and curious shadows; being attentive to lapses, loops, odd shifts and spectral movements within some of the most nondescript settings. In this way, the writing opens to different registers of perception, intuitions, attuning to unpredictable or even random events, and glimmers around the edges of comprehension. While the ideas and situations I explore are imbricated in concrete circumstances and significant details, the book moves away from conventional approaches to research. In this light, rather than proceeding through argumentation or a case study format, I am engaging in a mode of critique and generation along the lines of Margaret Cohen's synopsis of gothic Marxism:

> A notion of critique moving beyond logical argument and the binary opposition to a phantasmagorical staging more closely resembling psychoanalytic therapy, privileging non-rational forms of 'working through' and regulated by overdetermination rather than dialectics.
>
> (Cohen 1995, 11)

While having aspects of argumentation and detailed investigations of sites, the book has been assembled to slip past some of the usual trajectories into less certain terrain and more fruitful modes of understanding; and related to this, attempts to pull away from some limits of conventional political reason. Think of it as a very partial guide to political imaginations and strange temporality in the twenty-first century, charting the contours of eerie spaces, the inner workings of boredom and partial ruins. It is oriented to the question of the future and temporal imaginations, but it engages this often through a close investigation of space and psychosocial atmospheres. In alignment with this, the writing is conducive to a certain associative logic and moving in necessarily disparate ways. The unity is therefore distributive and malleable—engagement with temporality and possibility is distributed across three main chapters (logistics, boredom and obsolescence) which are comprised of short essays, vignettes and aphoristic sections. Concepts (around futurity and inevitability, novelty and outmodedness) and dynamics are revisited at different points and contexts, each time working through various facets. There is a heuristic drive more than economical exegesis of topics. The intention is to build into the analysis some room to move, at times leaping or reversing direction. Although at the risk of what might be seen as meandering at certain points, this allows a more inclusive, heterodoxic approach.

Overall, the approach I am taking is that futural impulses begin many times before what is normally identified as the future. Let's be practical—the future begins through conditions, refusals, sparks of supposed impossibility and social dreams. This is what makes the future possible, and it isn't the entrepreneurial 'be the future you want to be' or the empty ad copy that 'the future stars here' which is really just a forward projection of the present. This book is really a preface for a book on the future. Coming before the future is not the present or the past, but a condition that allows it, a futurity before the future. It is probably more helpful to think of beginnings—here comprised of conducive temporality in atmospheres and landscapes. The future is as much a question of instigations, often very distant preparations for the implementation of life forms, as it is something that is yet to happen.

Space-time ploys: motifs and tactics for exploration

As stated, this is not the kind of exploration that proceeds through the deployment of off-the-shelf research methods into case studies; instead ideas and sites are explored through ploys mainly developed around forms of suspension—a search for a savoir faire of how to investigate temporal imaginations within space-time crystallisations.

Rather than currents of time travel or flows of time from past into futures (always movement whether this is accelerated modern time, the flow of the river, arrows of time), a zone of possibility is explored in paused states or temporal dilations. This runs contrary to a tendency in contemporary cultural theory which, more often than not, associates flow with forms of emancipation, potential, subversion, etc. (lines of flight, undoing); and fixity is almost always synonymous with domination, commodification or imperialism (reification, territorialisation, reductionism). In the face of this tendency, the notion that political imaginations might be activated through suspension will sound counter-intuitive. These ploys, though not always directly labelled in the three main chapters, comprise a dynamic which is recurrent throughout the book—logistics (déjà vu moments, eerie suspensions), boredom (novelty and waste grind to a halt in the nullity of boredom) and Kitsault (a town frozen in time).

There is a paradoxical dynamic and a risk in exploring possibilities for agency in what appears to be intense moments of stasis. Capitalist temporality itself can be seen as a kind of arrested development—defined as a 'frenetic standstill' (Rosa 2013, 56), 'changing to remain the same' (Chun 2017) or in the fragmented temporality in everyday life in twenty-first century. Why break, brake or desynchronise, it might be asked, when the basis of ordinary experience in the twenty-first-century social life and its media environments is already built upon countless weird shifts in time, temporal fragmentations and incoherences? Because these 'natural' incoherences are experienced as more or less coherent non-events. Disjunctures are denied and experienced as seamless normality. Disruptions have been deeply assimilated and turned into the unremarkable flow of everyday life. The distinctions between the stasis of the continual present and the standstills I am rendering should become clear in the way the book is an active search for a certain savoir faire of how to enter alternate temporalities through forms of suspension. The deliberate cultivation of pauses is within a critical analytic and an attempt to fashion these cessations as eventful, points of fascination where we might see the anamorphosis (a distorted projection requiring the viewer to occupy a specific vantage point) of capitalism outside the normal viewpoint.

Particular ploys that are deployed directly and indirectly throughout the book include slipstreaming, lapsing, the dissolving view and cessations of novelty-obsolescence.

Slipstreaming

To elucidate this ploy, consider this statement by Fredric Jameson:

> We may pause to observe the way in which so much of left politics today—unlike Marx's own passionate commitment to a streamlined

technological future—seems to have adopted as its slogan Benjamin's odd idea that revolution means pulling the emergency brake on the runaway train of History, as though an admittedly runaway capitalism itself had the monopoly on change and futurity.

(Jameson quoted in Noys 2014, 83)

Lamenting a left that is reactive and can only aspire to mitigate social damage, Jameson invokes the idea of a streamlined future. Benjamin Noys, in a critique of accelerationism[1] which he sees as both resurgent and highly problematic, finds Jameson's exhortation of profound political change through the advancement of a technological future questionable and instead asserts the importance of this 'odd idea' of the emergency brake—a radical politics from the potentials of interruption and stoppage beyond mere defensive responses. The ideas and situations I am examining involve a politics of stoppage, and yet also work through a kind of streaming that is not onto the silver rails of the technological future, but rather, into a slipstreaming movement. This is derived from Bruce Sterling's idea (1989) of a way forward when science fiction seemed like a 'sprawling possessor of a dream that failed', obsolete like a 'contemporary Soviet Union'. It had drained away its energy and hung motionless. Slipstreaming begins within this suspension and genre confusion. It allows a way to edge beyond science fiction yet still move within its light (saving the genre by slipping past it). It usually involves a very gradual slip from faithful, matter-of-fact clarity to non-realistic strangeness. '[S]omething in the nature of an inherent dementia. These are fantastic elements which are not clear-cut "departures from known reality" but ontologically part of the whole mess; "real" compared to what?' (1989) Slipstreaming has the objective of 'mak[ing] you feel very strange; the way that living in the late twentieth century makes you feel' (1989). I am wrestling not with the genre of science fiction but with the conventions of cultural theory and academic analysis; and the objective is the strangeness of a basic feeling of twenty-first-century living. The writing works through a slipstreaming dynamic that begins in rather matter-of-fact descriptions and frameworks, and gradually skews terms and activates different registers.

Lapsing

This ploy merges the two main definitions of the word. In one sense, lapse refers to the interval between times and a leap across it. We lapse from one moment to the next, but the lapse is actually the time that has disappeared. What if we seek to enter the space of such a leap as a way of opening our experience of social and cultural process? Time lapse is a product of not only the difference of speed (between recording and viewing), but also a mechanism for representing temporal flow through the elision of time. The intervals vanish so we can see what would normally be imperceptible. I understand the lapse as that which is lost between the frames, a gap that is overcome in the acceleration of playback. What if we moved into these elisions themselves, what would space look like? What is needed is a technique for entering the lapses themselves, not their removal in the spectacularised flow of time. In a second sense, a lapse means some kind of failure or expiration has occurred, such as a lapse of concentration, membership, 'lapsed Catholic,' etc. A tactic of the book is to facilitate lapses—those of the usual temporal registers, letting slide the requisite pacing of contemporary subjective experience. The chapters detail instances of lapsing directly and indirectly, voluntarily and involuntarily. They produce ideas through lapse thinking which combines aspects of both falling out of a normal mode, as well as a positive kind of lapse in which disappearances and expiration enhance perceptions and understanding rather than manifesting decline.

The dissolving view (background activation)

The Paul Virilio quotation at the beginning of this Introduction is from *The Aesthetics of Disappearance* (2009) which is about the relation between forms of suspension and problematic distinctions between what is conventionally deemed as consequential and incidental—what I refer to in this book as low-density culture. Virilio is interested in a form of suspension that arises from a state of absence from the normal flow of time defined as 'picnolepsy', which is a mild seizure when one is pulled away from the external world in a movement breaking the quotidian flow of normal perception. The condition describes a particular disconnection from reality and a falling away from the oversaturated present. However, according to Virilio, this is not just a case of having maladapted consciousness, rather, such disruptions—disappearances—are in fact a foundation of perception in modern societies. Yet they are usually not acknowledged, but instead overcome by speed and re-presented as the real. This results in a mode of '[p]erception as made of breaks, absences, dislocations as well as by the capacity to produce patchworks of various contingent worlds' (Crary cited in Virilio 2009, 11). In pre-modern societies, these instances of seizure were understood in terms of trances, possession or reveries, and often involved the generation of insights; however in modern times, such lapsed states are themselves normalised and have become the basis of a symbolic order produced by gaps and breaks from perception (what for Virilio culminates in a culture of speed), yet with a total erasure of these stoppages and openings. Power operates in how such pauses and absence are filled in and made productive, and this is imbricated in hierarchies of value and significance.

So how to cultivate against smoothing over the picnoleptic in order that we might depart from sequential time and arrive at a kairos, an instant of 'opportunity' (45)? One way into this is through a particular immersion into the infra-ordinary, a preoccupation in this book, in experiences, landscapes and images which are likely to be seen as incidental. We could call these background studies, linked to a version of media ecology. The idea lies in an investment with what would be normally designated as a background, and looking for a kind of background activation; while at the same time viewing supposed focal points (objects, signs, buildings, etc.) as themselves a background. Instead of foregrounds and backgrounds, everything is within the milieu and its various modulations. The background thus gains a peculiar agency, within a 'dissolving view' (47) overturning the 'imposture of the immediate' (48). I explore logistical zones, boredom and outmodedness as possible areas for activation within what are usually seen as incidental backgrounds—backdrops for urban life and the excitement of commodities (in logistics); a haze from which arises content and stimulation (in boredom); and the outmoded and discarded as a vague mass from which the new surfaces (in Kitsault).

Cessations of novelty-obsolescence

A strong current in this book lies in ways of seeing the new within outmodedness, and vice versa—effectively to see them as two faces of same force—and exploring how a kind of futurity may begin through the cessation of novelty-obsolescence. This is a possibility arising not from waste per se (such as in the retro-futurist tendency in the work of artist Zoe Beloff, the ideas in Garnet Hertz and Jussi Parikka's 'Zombie Media' (2012) or the apocalypse-temporality of Evan Calder Williams' salvagepunk (2011)) but from seeing outside of novelty-obsolescence cycles altogether. This ploy involves an engagement with some fundamental aspects of modern temporality. 'Obsolescence is fundamental to the experience of modernity, not simply one dimension of an economic system' (Tischleder and Wasserman 2015). As such, it cannot be confined to the vestigial or out-of-date material, but fundamental to culture and society. The relentless forces of modernity produce waste and novelty within the same temporal band—two expressions of the same social substance. Flowing one way, innovation is produced, or switching the current into obsolescence (as Robert Smithson would have it in his 'ruins in reverse' (1996, 72)). Wendy Chun has examined a similar dynamic in the formulation that '[n]ew media exist at the bleeding edge of obsolescence' (2016, 1).

Within this view, what is called the outmoded is in actual fact a storage of a set of perplexing energies mutually constitutive of the new; and I look to suspensions of the novelty-obsolescence cycle so intrinsic to capitalist social life. The connection to obsolescence in the Kitsault and boredom chapters is relatively direct. Kitsault is a town frozen in time. Abandoned shortly after its construction in 1979, yet preserved and unused. It is almost a showroom of 'new' material culture from the late 1970s, and at the same time a dazing example of an almost complete environment of outmodedness. It perfects yet betrays the logic of the obsolete, and its temporality is complex, eerie and rife with strange banal energies. My approach to boredom is as a state of waste from which novel forms emerge (to escape the tedium), and yet inevitably dissolve back into it. Boredom is a universal solvent of modernity—cycles of new and old fall and rise from its grey core. The chapter on logistic spaces—almost always spaces built within the past two decades, and often in the past few years—would initially seem as having little to do with ideas related to obsolescence. They are the zones of digital infrastructure, the distribution centres for online shopping, the sites which allowed the society to function during the Covid-19 pandemic when everything else seemed to be closed or forbidden. These spaces are usually in newly developed ex-urban areas, thus an emergent form of post-urban space. However, as most of these spaces are built with lifespans of no more than 25 years, the spectre of their outmodedness is very apparent. The thrust of my ideas is that this 'new' is inextricable from its imminent fate as an obsolete form, all the more so in the way these spaces are so closely linked with fast-moving technological development. In Walter Benjamin's words—one of the most pre-eminent cultural theorists of suspension—'[i]n the convulsions of the commodity economy we begin to recognise the monuments of the bourgeoisie as ruins even before they have crumbled' (Benjamin 1999, 13).

While not directly applying Benjamin's practice of dialectics at a standstill, the explorations and discussion in the subsequent chapters work through a vocabulary informed by Benjamin's thinking on temporal alignments within arrested instances. His 'anti-continuism', as Jameson calls it (Jameson 2020, 230), is not a mere counter-intuitive technique of cultural theory, but with the revolutionary aim: 'to interrupt the course of the world' (Benjamin 2003, 170). Within this politics, it is paramount to see beyond a simple equation of fluidity being synonymous with action (or even vitality) and suspension as inaction (or even breakdown and demise). Thus Jameson encapsulates Benjamin's concept of the standstill in the following way.

> The frozen moment does not bring the action to an end; rather, it allows us to analyse it into multiple outcomes, . . . on the basis of a fundamental situation, a shared dilemma, which the arrest of movement reveals and produces, beyond all distraction, like an X-ray.
>
> (Jameson 2020, 230)

Of particular importance in this motionless view is the place Benjamin gives to astonishment in the entanglement of past and present, novelty and detritus (when the fluid or amorphous is transformed into a still and surprising form). In a process partly derived from Surrealism with its aim of dissolving social fate, in the standstill we arrive at 'the site at which the dream images come undone' (Roy 2011, 16), where the harmonious façade of everyday life and its implacable sense of inevitability is dislocated affecting a blow on reality.

The missing double introduction

Because this is about exploring temporal disturbances as political prospect, rousing political imaginations not by the great vista of the future but through lapsing and entanglements of time and material, it is best to begin a book like this with a double introduction. Two similar, overlapping introductions, which are not fully aware of each other, in a book with its door ajar. A multiverse introduction—many of the same ideas and components are doubled but some key differences become apparent as they unfold as if through a slightly different gene sequence. Variation of a similar, but they perform the same function. There is no definitive way in, opening with such variance. What does this have to do with the future, with temporal politics, special points of suspension? Between the two introductions is a gap. In spite of my best intentions and efforts, my thinking will be predictable or even plodding, so it makes sense to open a different kind of space, not hypothetical. I may try to cover up that gap, disguising it as an accidental incoherence, something 'beyond the scope of this investigation,' or just blame it on absent-mindedness. But maybe it is a rift in the here and now.

There was a second introduction, but I can't find it anymore. However, there is a residual version in the existing repetitions. The plan was to work with this doubling, to allow multiple tracks of a set of ideas. *Before the Future*, the multiverse edition, an intervention into the empty time of expert academic studies; a hope that it would emerge out of a heterogeneous time. It contained a transcription of a recording of a hypnotised voice which seemed to speak out of the essence of the main ideas of the book—what Kitsault really is, what is really going on in those distribution centres, pure messianic boredom. But I can't find this variation, and presumably they can't find this one. A confounding overlap—you would be uncertain which one you were reading, which one you were in. When this book hits a fluctuation, a déjà vu, it would be like it has encountered another time (contemporaneous or from a past or future, some different place altogether), and this second preface would be a way into this, at least an acknowledgement. But it is not here—lapse of memory, perhaps it never existed, just a figment. It was going to make all the difference—unseat this one, with a level of nuance and profundity missing here. Is it the hedged preface—the way the book should have gone and a signal that I knew it, the 'shorted' version I can point to and say, I agree, and this shows I understood all of that? Haunted by it, I have nevertheless decided not to reconstruct it. May this be the version that disappeared from the other preface? There are words in it apologizing for the missing second introduction, which is the one you are reading. Different sets of readers are wondering about this one, how it disappeared, what were the intriguing subtle differences that might bring the whole thing to life. In any case, the introduction is at least doubled when read.

Writing as preventing future loss

Writing this as if it was something that had already happened in some other time (perhaps a future, perhaps something else), and brought to light just before it would have been lost for good—found somewhere, reclaimed, not from an actual landfill but in the places leading up to it, the piles, corners and stuff, in a PDF in an oddly named folder on a memory stick or on a forgotten WordPress blog. Forgotten but then found, as if only through this lost-and-found conversion it could not only be saved but produced in the right way. More likely, it is actually from a near future. Written from the not outlandish premonition of seeing it abandoned. Therefore, writing in this way is pre-empting a loss, staving it off, and hence making a future. Seeing this tendency—writing as intercepting a discard from another time—on a collective or at least supra-individual level, a cultural wish. Writing this as if I was reading it from out of there. One's ideas separated in time, either backwards or forward, the words might be hard to see but the scene is so easily imagined. Uncanny duplication, not as if someone else, or something else, had written it; but like something partially forgotten, recognised only when seeing it again as it is written. It is not like an idealised image appears through this ricochet, a marvel of time that puts an idea inside resin. More like a kind of textual reverb so that ideas take on this processing otherwise they would be flat, merely assertions, more lines of theory, analysis of media and culture to be made searchable, more content to be assessed and dispensed with. Does it make it worse that writing must not only fulfil the requirements but also sound like it echoed in the right way, pulled out of time? A time warp gimmick as the only way to beat the inevitability of detritus?

Strange politics, weird left

Part of the inspiration for the approaches of this book comes from Afrofuturism which offers some of the strongest currents of rethinking the politics of time. Acknowledging my subject position as a white person, I'm struck by the conviction and expansiveness of its concepts which exceed a lot of the existing forms of critical analysis. Examples of its salience include Kodwo Eshun's (2003) assessment that corporate business power operates through the endorsement of its future interests, which become the dominant terms of imagining the future while masking present realities. The management of the temporal unknown and the attempt to conquer it through predictive technologies and business determinism forms the basis of chronopolitical struggles in the twenty-first century. Thus power lies in claiming the plausibility of what is to come. Afrofuturism's 'extraterrestrial turn' (298)—outer space as a zone for recasting the history of enslavement and encountering different worlds to come—challenges this management of time and opens a space for transvaluation and creative speculation. The complex temporalities explored by the art collective Black Quantum Futurism (Phillips 2016) are a further articulation of this. Their projects involve combinations of African and African-American traditions, quantum physics and aesthetic futurism embedded in local struggles and mixings of time and space.

The necessity of getting beyond a limited pool of intellectual resources also led me to what can be called 'the weird left' comprised of a loose assembly of ideas associated with acid communism (Fisher 2018; Gilbert 2019), publications and podcasts like the *Locust Review*, Stephen Duncombe's dream politics (2019) and critical irrealism (Löwy 2009). These are more recent expressions of a longer convergence between Marxism, liberational movements and an openness to the non-rational;

as well as aspects of cultural theory veering towards mysticism such as in the aforementioned gothic Marxism related to Walter Benjamin, Georges Bataille, Surrealism, and further back into nineteenth-century utopians like Charles Fourier. Contemporary weird left thinking, some of which move through provocative coinage or even joke terms, is specific to a particular historical moment intensifying onward from the 2007 financial crisis, and developed through a response to the Trump presidency, the mainstreaming of far-right movements, the circumstances of the Covid-19 pandemic, and inspired by the Black Lives Matter movement. The main impetus is the desire for an inclusion of irrational, intuitive and affective elements into leftist politics, especially not yielding these as the sole domain of far-right populism and conspiracy theories. A component of it is also to move beyond the legacy of post-war social democracy (the Keynesian horizon of socio-economic possibility), technocratic centrism and the urgent necessity of expanding the imaginative base of politics against a twenty-first century TINA dogma (There Is No Alternative to capitalism and (il)liberal individualism) and zombie neoliberalism in the face of all of their failings. As well, the views and attitudes that fall under what I am calling the weird left counter certain strictures of 'criticality' and question whether the orthodoxies of conventional academic work are capable of producing vibrant intellectual currents and experiments. Connecting this book with such heady sounding tags and sub-movements might create expectation for what is in fact a rather clear-headed, subtle kind of weird; however, this is actually in keeping with the spirit of this weird left which engages with certain esoteric elements and 'out there' notions, but is nevertheless generally grounded in cultural history and socio-economic analysis. There is a concern that working under the heading of 'weird' would be to denigrate one's ideas or perform a kind of amusement act in relation to a perceived stultified world of serious scholarly work (playing other to their same). Perhaps the best way to encapsulate the spirit of this approach comes from Gargi Bhattacharyya's (2021) invocation of the importance of being ridiculous in a time of inculcated despair. She asserts that the general cultural and political climate promulgated over the past several decades in the West has trained populations to lower expectations, and governs through a kind of engineered despair (which encompasses forms of 'excitement' which can only ever occur within tracks that reaffirm existing limits and interests).

Mark Fisher is a key figure in this weird left approach. A frequent response to his writings on capitalist realism, and his work more generally, is that it is so bleak, leaving little in the way of affirmation and creative initiatives. This may be a misinformed criticism because it does not consider the breath of Fisher's ideas, in particular, his unfinished project Acid Communism (2018, 776–797), his writings on hauntology and *The Weird and Eerie* (2016). My supposition is that this later text explores the notion (at least implicitly) that strange temporality has come to function in the place of the future in political imaginations. Futural energy and its horizon have been dispersed and reappear in different spaces and forms. This idea lies at the crux of my investigations and which I will further introduce in the second part of the Introduction.

But for the moment, let us remain with acid communism, a term coined by Fisher in a proposal for an unfinished book.

> It is a joke of sorts, but one with very serious purpose. It points to something that, at one point, seemed inevitable, but which now appears impossible: the convergence of class consciousness, socialist-feminist consciousness-raising and psychedelic consciousness, the fusion of new social movements with a communist project, an unprecedented aestheticisation of everyday life.
>
> (2018, 782)

The ideas around acid communism are rooted in the 1960s and 70s counterculture and political radicalism, and it is both a call for a reactivation of this past and a ghostly projection of this onto the future as an unfinished movement. In many ways for Fisher, it is a continuation of the psycho-social insurrection of the 1960s which he sees as blocked by a neoliberal counter-revolution; however, what happened in the 1960s and 70s was just the first attempt at acid communism. The fact that such a proposition is likely to be dismissed as 'just the 60s' is itself indicative of a dominant political order which aggressively maintains the depletion (or domestication) of this movement. Engaging with the radical collectivity, scope and confidence of this earlier movement is 'less an act of remembering than of unforgetting, a counter-exorcism of the spectre of a world which could be free. Acid Communism is the name I have given to this spectre' (781).

The term, then, refers to the possibilities of a radical movement rather than a championing of drug-taking or hedonistic excess. The psychedelic view is essential, yet should be seen within the political project of altering the relationship to what is experienced as reality. 'If the very fundamentals of our experience, such as our sense of space and time, can be altered, does that not mean that the categories by which we live are plastic, mutable?' (789) Psychedelics here fall in a terrain of struggle around fundamental constitution of social life, and the politics of its envisioning and reconstruction, and hallucinatory explorations occur in Fisher's 'sober Spinozist sense' (Colquhoun 2020). Acid communism is a call to reverse the consciousness deflation of capitalist realism, and activate psychic and symbolic resources to break the existing sociopolitical monopolisation of social life.

I connect with these currents, especially in the need to counter climates of psychic deflation and making current inevitabilities impossible. But how weird are the situations and ideas I am exploring in this book—rabbit holes, nightmares, the fifth dimension? It is pretty mundane, and if there is an esoteric vibe here it is of a very low intensity. It is about logistical spaces, a generic town and boredom after all. In fact, that is the strangeness on offer—to go into the banal to the point where reality appears slightly altered, a blur which creeps into nondescript landscapes; deconstruct-ing the normal by means of passing it directly into its grey heart; into an eeriness that lies in blanks and seemingly ordinary experience. Bloch struggled against a 'terrible banalization' (1988, 3) of utopia as it was con-fined within blueprints and the promises of consumerism (we can think of the enduring image of General Motors' Futurama or the contemporary examples of Amazon's Alexa or billionaire space adventures), but perhaps within the banal itself—at least in some of its weird provinces—abides a utopian element. This is not the weird that drives one back to comfortable, safe environments and equates the unknown with doom; rather an eeriness that moves towards something like a future. 'In a sense, there is no word for the other side of the eerie, this dispassionate positive side of the eerie is precisely what's been edited out of the world' (Justin Barton in Barcelos et al. 2007, 84).

Part II: From cancelled futures to the eerie

In this exploration of the possibilities of eerie banality, it is necessary to work back to why such strange framing is required in the first place. My interest in disquieting atmospheres that might stir temporal imaginations is hopefully clear at this point, but the assertion that we need recourse to rather esoteric sounding notions because the future has been cancelled needs clari-fication. As well, how am I defining some of the key terms around temporal politics? This section addresses these concerns and provides a theoretical basis for thinking strange times, in particular, the heterochronic undoing of the present which will serve as a groundwork for the explorations in the chapters that follow.

This book was initially *going to be* another missive on 'lost futures.' The absence of the future is very apparent in terms of a political paralysis in the face of the climate crisis, growing socio-economic inequality, the vilification of refugees, a proliferation of walls and surveillance and unfortunately much more. In the early twenty-first century, at least in the West, there is an almost automatic pessimism towards what is to come, and the only optimism left is mainly for those benefiting from the absence of the future. That part of the equation—the lack of futurity—is clear; however, what is the future in this narrative of the cancelled future and are there other anticipatory imaginaries we should be looking at instead? In the first place, this lost future is a modern, primarily a twentieth-century version; and I became increasingly ambivalent about it. I will work through this in more detail, but David Graeber provides an initial encapsulation in 'Of Flying Cars and the Declining Rate of Profit' (2012):

> A secret question hovers over us, a sense of disappointment, a broken promise we were given as children about what our adult world was supposed to be like. I am referring not to the standard false promises that children are always given (about how the world is fair, or how those who work hard shall be rewarded), but to a particular generational promise—given to those who were children in the fifties, sixties, seventies, or eighties—one that was never quite articulated as a promise but rather as a set of assumptions about what our adult world would be like. And since it was never quite promised, now that it has failed to come true, we're left confused: indignant, but at the same time, embarrassed at our own indignation, ashamed we were ever so silly to believe our elders to begin with. Where, in short, are the flying cars? Where are the force fields, tractor beams, teleportation pods, antigravity sleds, tricorders, immortality drugs, colonies on Mars, and all the other technological wonders any child growing up in the mid-to-late twentieth century assumed would exist by now? Even those inventions that seemed ready to emerge—like cloning or cryogenics—ended up betraying their lofty promises. What happened to them? (66)

I am heir to this disappointment, and I too have wondered at certain points about the antigravity we were sort of promised. Aside from its disappearance or betrayal, how enthralling is this vision of the future? The quote is from a piece Graeber wrote for *The Baffler* magazine which is for a general audience and not a rigorous study, but I think it is nevertheless a serious expression of a very pervasive image of how the future is imagined, expected, and moreover, longed for. Yet in many ways, this future doesn't seem very futuristic because it is so deeply and faithfully committed to a Western post-war extractivist imaginary, which is at once overly 'futuristic' (in the sense of residing within progress modern myths, sequential advancement of the new, within a residual flying car, *Jetsons* futurism); and because of this predetermination, not very futuristic at all. Perhaps we must lose the future in order to have one. But it is already gone, of course. I don't mean only the ongoing eradication of the future of the continual present, rather, there is something in the narrative of the lost future with its impasses and stasis which is itself a cul-de-sac. Lose the lost future, then? Let the dead bury the dead, forward, accelerate? Some desperate relaunch of the future as a reaction to a lost condition doesn't have much prospect either, unless it is an endless future of trauma and obliviousness. Not only is it impossible to eradicate such absences and a sense of loss, but this dimension is where certain futurities might begin. But these dramatic, contradictory speculations and leaps are too soon, moving too quickly, let's slow this down perhaps even to a standstill. All this future talk needs to circle back to the crucial questions of political myths and what is meant by impasses of futural imaginations and the future itself.

The approach I am exploring in this book is of a temporal politics not based on a progressive confidence in the future but one that arises from temporalising outside the dominant terms which undermine the containment of the present. I came to see that systemic alterity, an enthralment of what lies beyond existent social life begins in alternate temporality—strange time, eeriness, processes of counter-temporalising. If this sounds like a futural politics through other means, by different conceptions and modalities, maybe a cryptic reinvention of the future, then you have understood correctly. But this is hopefully not just a smoke-and-mirrors reappearance of the future; instead, these other means, conceptions and rearticulations of temporal possibility are the future itself, however partial and indistinct. This second section of the introduction moves through this assertion and explores these terms and ideas.

It must be stressed that by proceeding through a politics of time I am in no way oblivious to space. This is not a vision of time over space (as in a simplified rendering of Virilio gives us a true champion of time over space (see Klinke 2013) or a caricatured Marxian annihilation of space by time). All of the explorations in the following chapters involve interrogations of spaces (logistic spaces, the zones of boredom, the town of Kitsault); however, I am exploring a temporal avenue into these. It is pointless to separate time from space, yet it can be energising to follow a temporal current through spaces. Rather than an obliteration of space into time—a move which as Dorine Massy comprehensively stated 'impoverishes the temporal' (Massey 2005, 89)—there is a temporal invested entry into space.

Myths of the lost future

'As for the future, which may still be alive in some small heroic collectivities on the Earth's surface, it is for us either irrelevant or unthinkable' (Jameson 2005, 287–288). Such a conviction is not unique to Jameson, indeed there is a consensus among certain cultural and social theorists—the presumed 'us' in his declaration (examples might include Fisher 2014; Berardi 2011; Crary 2013; Nowotny 2005; Auge 2015; Bauman 2017)—that the future as collective possibility has fallen, and this is the result of the following narrative that marks a dramatic change in temporal frameworks and a stifling of historical forces. Modern temporality was shaped by a dynamic split between current conditions and conceptualisations and a future time. In Reinhart Koselleck's (2004) terms, a gap exists between experience and the horizon of expectations. In a modern society, subjects expect what they have not experienced; and this gap becomes dynamic and a basis of politics. Experiences and circumstances change and accelerate, and this potential difference between now and a futural condition animates various political projects. This forward orientation and disjunction between current experience and anticipation generates the drive for social change and functions as a basis for the concept of revolution, leftist political projects, as well as a conservatism born out of resisting the effects of acceleration.

The second part of this narrative (following David Cunningham 2015) is that the meaning of acceleration has changed dramatically by the end of the twentieth century—things haven't slowed as much as there is acceleration without the alterity of the future or a gap between experience and expectation. The fall of this temporal dynamic undermines futural politics as they have been structured over the past several centuries in the West, while at the same time, as Peter Osborne (2011) has observed, there is a residual over-investment in the promise of the new and in expecting the unexpected. This has resulted in cultures of instantaneity, of which Paul Virilio has written about extensively, presenting a strong case of historical paralysis of the continual present. Contemporary society, in a range of different global contexts, has a frenzied sense of change that does not lead to a qualitatively different time. Broken off from political modernism, contemporary acceleration 'become[s] the mark not of "progress" but of the paradoxical temporality of a "frenetic standstill"' (Rosa 2013, 56).

Following on from this, in lieu of the dynamism of futurist projects, there is a sense of diminished expectations in contemporary society—younger generations facing declining prospects and a bewildering array of environmental, economic and geopolitical crises forming a 'present without a view' (Danowski and Viveiros de Castro 2017, 5). And low expectations often flip into the anticipation that the worst is yet to come. In place of a future of a better world lies peril, evidenced by an incessant flow of apocalyptic television programmes, films and novels (the future as dread, collapse and apocalypse: *Life Without People*, *Walking Dead*, *Interstellar*, *Hunger Games*). In a dire revision of Alfred North Whitehead,[2] society becomes dangerous without a future, and a politics of paralysis appears to have developed to exploit this which can be seen in the inaction on climate change, the inability to address the refugee crisis, and in post-financial crisis economic decline. In contending with financial uncertainty, insecure employment and housing, large sections of the population live with a 'damaged future' (Butler 2012), or a collectively mortgaged future. It is not hard to make the case that the current rise of reactionary political movements are but an expression of the fall of the political future.

Cancelled futures

To move into this further, I will consider accounts of the lost left future in more detail in Franco Berardi and Mark Fisher. This line of thinking, I want to stress, is one that I consider as formative but nevertheless problematic and needs to be recast. Franco Berardi's *After the Future* (2011) is a strong, evocative version of a lost future narrative, which is a book about the collapse of the imagination of the future from the perspective of a breakdown of subjectivity. The future is defined and explored primarily as a powerful political myth of the twentieth century, and one that sustained movements of all kinds. This is certainly not Berardi's last word on futurity either, with *Futurability: The Age of Impotence and the Horizon of Possibility* (2017) taking a somewhat different tack of exploring futural attributes. Nevertheless, the ideas expressed in *After the Future* portray a futureless contemporary condition and function as a clear reference to think through the problem of the future in the twenty-first century. Perhaps it is even, optimistically, more of a historical document of a time that we have left and entered a somewhat different climate for the politics of time—for better and for worse.

After the Future, a collection of essays themed around the perilous condition of living without the future, is often most compelling in its diagnosis of the psycho-pathologies of neoliberalism than theorising the future, however for Berardi, the two are inextricably linked. But what is meant by the future? To start with, the future in *After the Future* is almost synonymous with twentieth-century modernism, hence 'the century that trusted in the future.' (15) For Berardi, this future is based on 'the cultural situation of progressive modernity, the cultural expectations that were fabricated during the long period of modern civilization, reaching a peak after the Second World War.' (18) In this light, it is a future evidently based on the past, very specific to a European narrative, unabashedly united under the banner of progress. 'Moderns are those who live time as the sphere of a progress towards perfection, or at least towards improvement, enrichment, and rightness' (21). In more detail,

> In the modern era the future was imagined thanks to metaphors of progress. Scientific research and economical entrepreneurship in the

centuries of modern development were inspired by the idea that knowledge will lead to an ever more complete mastery of the human universe. The Enlightenment sanctions this conception, and positivism makes of it an absolute belief. The Marxist revolutionary ideologies, guided by an historicist and dialectical vision, also imagine the future on the basis of a progressive teleological model. The present contains, in the form of contradiction, a potential that history is necessarily destined to resolve. It is from the dialectical solution of present contradictions that a social form free from poverty and war will be born. This form is what the Marxist movement calls communism. In the last part of the 20th century these philosophical premises disintegrated. But what has disappeared, more than anything else, is the credibility of a progressive model for the future.

(59)

Berardi is, along with Graeber and Fisher, propounding the loss of the future in autobiographical and generational terms: 'My generation grew up at the peak of this mythological temporalization, and it is very difficult, maybe impossible, to get rid of it, and look at reality without this kind of temporal lens. I'll never be able to live in accordance with the new reality, no matter how evident, unmistakable, or even dazzling.' (19) This contributes to a self-fulfilling condition—unless you were born in a certain time and space, you will never have the future which required coming of age within specific 'cultural expectations' (18) shaped by this ideology of advancement and endless growth.

The modern future was, according to Berardi, reassuring because it could be known by tracing its linear direction and through scientific means—whether the laws of human evolution or the motion of the planets. It also instilled confidence because it could be directed and transformed 'by human will, by industry, economic technique and political action. . . . The 20th century trusted in the future because it trusted in scientists who foretold it, and in policy makers able to make rational decisions.' (51) People were not at the mercy of a fatalistic future but one that was collectively constructed, clearly understood and encoded into social institutions.

Berardi's real emphasis is on the experience and composition of subjectivity within this temporal narrative. This was imbricated, in part, in a political left version of the twentieth-century modern futurism which enabled a collective consciousness and a feeling that not only can things be changed and different views of the world realised but this can be done on a radical scale both in terms of a spatial-social horizon and in far-reaching timelines. Yet this future is a politically ambivalent myth, producing utopias and dystopias, dreams and nightmares—although with Berardi, the worst nightmare seems to be the end of modern future rather than its devastation of mechanised war, Bhopal and Chernobyl, the Holocaust, human-made climate change and so on. The progressive future was an imaginary through which all major ideologies of the nineteenth to twentieth centuries aligned themselves to (bourgeois capitalism, fascism, Soviet communism), as well as the major social movements of this time. This futurism has all the familiar components of endless economic growth, continually rising standards of livings and extending knowledge. Berardi is frank in acknowledging the link between progressive modernism and colonialism, the depletion of natural resources and the fact that this political myth could as well lead to fascism and devastation as it could to emancipation. His writing is both an indictment and celebration of modern faith in the future, but one thing is clear for him—without it, all manner of peril ensues.

For Berardi, progressive futurism became a victim of itself—its colonialism, extractivism and obsession with speed seemed productive until these external drives became internal to white western political subjects and their movements. At the end of the twentieth century, such modern drives began to devour even its proponents and its futural prospects, and as it reached its external limits, these futural energies then turned on the internal space of the human. Intensified through the ubiquity of networked technologies, this drive to speed and extraction formed the psychic roots of neoliberal pathologies. The machinic expansion so crucial to modern progress, when trained on the self, forced an acceleration resulting in a loss of sensitivity and empathy, and the decomposition of the subject altogether.

> Speed itself has been internalised. During the 20th century, the machine of speed accomplished the colonisation of global space; this was followed by the colonisation of the domain of time, of the mind and perception, so that the future collapsed. In the acceleration of psychic and cognitive rhythm is rooted the collapse of the future.
>
> (23)

Berardi's end of the future, which although he dates it to 1977 (the beginning of the end of the future), is even more endemic to the first decade of the 2000s—the time of the book was written—during a phase of digitally enhanced neoliberalism in which a confidence in the future was well and truly over. 'How will it be possible to create a collective consciousness in the age of precariousness and the fractalization of time?' (18) Life after the future is marked by 'the absence of an active culture, lack of a public sphere, void of collective imagination, palsy of the process of subjectivation. The way to build a conscious collective subject seems obstructed' (12).

Contrasting the contemporary 'fractalization' (8) of time, the political myth of the future (akin to religious belief) required speed and forward movement to sustain it, almost as if the commitment to continual motion was how one believed. 'The myth of speed sustained the whole edifice of the imaginary of modernity, and the reality of speed played a crucial role in the history of capital' (21). Slowness, then, is primarily an anti-futural force. The confidence in the future as condition of possibility ends most resolutely through deceleration. Imaginaries are incrementally overturned through a 'slow pervasion of the social mind' (37), in 'a self-fulfilling prophecy that has slowly enveloped the world' (12).

So how to have a future without the cult of speed, or in slow motion or even a standstill? Can there be slow futures? For the most part, slowness in *After the Future* takes on a decidedly pejorative or even destructive association; however, it concludes with a certain extolling of the virtues of life in the absence of speed in a political practice of exhaustion. Berardi questions the centrality of action and growth in so many different areas of social life, and especially in militant activism. Counter to this, he considers the merits of 'sensuous slowness' (158) and an idea of resignation ('facing the inevitable with a relaxed soul' (158)) as a refusal to participate in a capitalist social life defined by the imperative of continual participation, aggressive competition and engagement at all times. Instead of vistas of emancipatory futures and the recomposition of subjects, there is the attainment of a fullness and sensitivity to the present in life after the future. The means to this are through forms of withdrawal, escape and self-reliance (autonomy). 'We will sing to the infinity of the present and abandon the illusion of a future' (166). Berardi sees an openness of experience in this form of abandonment, but this is in no way connected to a futural imagination as there is a fundamental incompatibility between the slowness of such withdrawal and the dynamism of futurity. Radical decelerationism allows for the restoration of dignity and hope, but not the future.

For Berardi, then, there would seem to be no future outside of this forward blur which animates belief in what is to come. Similarly, how to know and produce the future without such reassuring linearity and scientific determination? This is precisely how I understand where current social imaginaries begin—a time to come outside the cult of speed and beyond progressive contours. In fact, the main intuition I am exploring in this book is a futurity, or a pre-future to be exact, not animated through speed but through the absence of motion. In this eerie calm comes a different imaginary. Sounds are ambient, in a landscape where buildings and marshes loom, where backgrounds shimmer within an atmosphere conducive to counter-temporalising.

'The Slow Cancellation of the Future': fisher's lost future

The question of slowness connects Berardi's ideas to Fisher. A chapter in Fisher's *Ghosts of My Life* is titled with Berardi's phrase 'the slow cancellation of the future' (2014, 2) where he elaborates on this condition marked by the total absence of a speedy succession of cultural styles and the general feeling of time going nowhere. Fisher is particularly oriented to how the future ends through slowness and gradualism, and such deceleration defines life hereafter. Gradualism itself is the process through which collective possibility and confidence in the future die, with the implicit, revolting metaphor of a frog dying in a slowly heated pot unable to perceive subtle change over time. Presumably, a fast cancellation would be easier to resist because of the emotive response generated out of this suddenness. Its energy could be redirected in keeping with social movements animated by speed. Instead neoliberalism—in consort with its more dramatic advances—does much of its radical work through relentless yet almost indiscernible transformation (about as exciting as watching the movement of the hour hand of a clock). It serves slow heavy lobs, inertial sludge, which zaps resistance and leaves baffled, deflated opponents with little to work with until the damage is seen in retrospect. Even realisations of this gradual regression are likewise slow, so slow they usually come after the fact, and of course, after the future.

Life after the future transpires without forward momentum, thus the twenty-first century is culturally marooned in the twentieth century as if it has yet to begin; however, this stalled condition nevertheless circulates its no longer new culture through ultra-fast data connections and 8K video. Hence it is culturally regressive within a hollowed-out current of technical advancement. All of this generally applied to the West, and very specific to the UK if not the English context leaving open larger questions of the applicability of this to other regions. For Fisher, the current historical moment is without cultural definition, and instead the early twenty-first century has an excessive tolerance of culture from the recent past. Nothing ever vanishes, instead culture languishes in a condition Simon Reynolds refers to as 'dyschronia'—we experience temporal disjunctures continually yet without any feeling of the uncanniness. 'Anachronism is now taken for granted' (19). The great succession of styles of Western modernity, driven forward through the centuries, has ground to a halt. 'Rather than the old recoiling from the 'new' in fear and incomprehension, those whose expectations were formed in an earlier era are more likely to be startled by the sheer persistence of recognisable forms' (16).

Fisher is insightful in detailing a futureless condition, but what is this future that no longer exists? Although he did not extensively theorise a philosophical basis of a concept of the future, there are nevertheless some core characteristics. As can be intimated by the anxiety around the easy acceptance of dyschronia and the loss of progressions of novel forms, the future is primarily understood as an engine of cultural development. Novel cultural forms, born out of their unique historical moments, are then displaced by other forms which are exploratory and moving towards expressions that exceed the existent. It is very much a linear force proceeding through a clear succession of styles, distinct from the previous and defining a specific present which is then displaced by the next. This is a futurity rooted in aesthetic experience and cultural movements—especially in music, film and literature. Exemplary in this was the future orientation of 'popular modernism' (24) in the UK spanning from the 1960s to the 80s comprising a cultural ecology of 'the music press and the more challenging parts of public service broadcasting,' as well as 'postpunk, brutalist architecture, Penguin paperbacks and the BBC Radiophonic Workshop' (24). This aesthetic futurism can be defined as a kind of accelerationism, at least as Fisher defines the term. 'Here we can turn to the vexed question of accelerationism. I want to situate accelerationism not as some heretical form of Marxism, but as an attempt to converge with, intensify, and politicise the most challenging and exploratory dimensions of popular culture' (Fisher 2013, 4). This version of accelerationism is based on the continually unprecedented overcoming of self-present limits of the human. Fisher quotes Foucault:

> The problem is not to recover our 'lost' identity, to free our imprisoned nature, our deepest truth; but instead, the problem is to move towards something radically Other. The centre, then, seems still to be found in Marx's phrase: man produces man. . . . For me, what must be produced is not man identical to himself, exactly as nature would have designed him or according to his essence; on the contrary, we must produce something that doesn't yet exist and about which we cannot know how and what it will be.
>
> (cited in Fisher 2013, 7)

An intriguing aspect of Fisher's idea of the future is that it is both accelerationist, in the above sense, and hauntological—in fact the early twenty-first century is haunted by this accelerationism. The popular modern mentioned is not a series of dead artefacts or fodder for a retro-futurist style, but an unfinished futural force that returns in the early twentieth century in a range of cultural expressions, especially in music. This futurity is active in the present, albeit as a haunting absence—a shadowy presence of a past accelerationism that is neither fully past nor contemporary. Thus the only way to be a futurist in the twenty-first century, at least in England, is by 'refusing to give up the ghost' (Fisher 2014, 24).

In this way, Fisher joins Berardi in an ambivalence around slowness and paused states. For the most part, a lack of forward movement and speed is tantamount to the end of future; yet Fisher's writing provides numerous accounts of fascinating instances of stalled temporality which are not impasses or expressions of paralysis but weird forces which undermine the containment of the present. However at other key points in Fisher's thinking, strange temporal states are synonymous with political stasis. In *Ghosts of My Life*, Fisher refers to an episode of a British sci-fi television programme *Sapphire and Steel* from the 1980s to illustrate the cancelled future condition. In the episode, the main characters are caught in a bizarre space that seems to be outside the flow of time. What is more, it is not only broken off from the normal flow of time but appears to have many different time periods jumbled together. 'As Sapphire and Steel's colleague Silver puts it "time just got mixed, jumbled up, together, making no sort of sense." Anachronism, the slippage of discrete time periods into one another, was throughout the series the major symptom of time breaking down' (15). This is what the cancellation of the future feels like, and the episode is illustrative of a temporal shutdown which began in the 1980s. The implication is that, seemingly, a time of cultural vibrancy and a strong futural politics would be one where time works correctly, with the minutes and years passing smoothly along a linear passage. It is almost as if we just need to iron out the jumbles, reassign the anachronisms back to their correct place in history. Temporal anomalies are, in this case at least, only a symptom of social pathology and political malaise. This is surprising not only as it appears to move against the hauntological resistance just mentioned (a major current in his writing) but also goes against the grain of a whole series of writing and insights he developed on temporal politics which explored the complexities of strange atmospheres—a temporal politics lying in unsettling time, unseating the presumptions of the dominant symbolic order of the present. Examples of this include the audio essay 'On Vanishing Land' with Justin Barton, *The Weird and the Eerie*, and various blog posts in K Punk. Fisher's writing is particularly fascinating when writing about temporal anomalies, uncanny zones, loops and a hetrochronia imbued with lucidity exceeding the enclosed present. But is Fisher's investment in hauntological temporality more a question of compensation or a holding futurity which would then be dispensed with the resumption of a progressive future last seen in the 1980s? We could finally give up the ghost and return to the true time of the future?

Herein lies a particularly frustrating aspect of both Berardi and Fisher's thinking on temporality and the question of the future. They are both insightful and evocative writers of the politics of time, yet there is a literal formulation that dulls a more vibrant dimension of their ideas—the future is synonymous with twentieth-century futurity, thus the twenty-first century is indeed after the future. It can easily feel like a foregone conclusion. Proceeding from such a historically and personally rooted conception of futurity— a time-signatured conception of possibility no less—how could forms of futurity ever thrive outside this original context? What are the prospects of a futurity based on doggedly hanging onto promises of the future experienced in an earlier phase of one's life, with the insinuation that engaging with other notions of the future would be something close to capitulation?

The 'lost future' perspective in both Berardi and Fisher is grounded in ambivalences which both look to temporal anomalies (haunted returns, suspensions, slowness) as an opening of imaginations, even functioning as a basis of a political practice, akin to yet in lieu of the future; yet they are also insistent that a time lacking a progressive forward drive is doomed, synonymous with the end of the future. My point here is not to expose a telling contradiction, rather, to move on the possibility that such slowness and jumbled temporality is not a morbid symptom or an after-image, but provides a pathway into temporal possibility and a different kind of futurity—a particular anticipatory mode and temporal practice separate from a linear flow of sequential developments. Both authors are presenting imaginative resources for releasing the constraints of the here and now in their examinations of exhausted time (in Berardi) or hauntology and eerie time (in Fisher), even as they are demonstrating impasses which render the future as impossible.

From the future to weird time

I am seizing on the question of slowness and temporal decomposition in Berardi and Fisher's ideas not because I am dedicated to deceleration (ideologies of slowness, degrowth, antagonisms towards technological development) but because it is an entry into temporal anomalies and heterochronic dynamics in thinking the future—an overture into weird temporality which might lead into experience outside of either acceleration or deceleration. Dale Carrico provides a useful distinction between futurity and The Future (which is highlighted by Eric C. H. de Bruyn and Sven Lütticken in the *Futures Report* (2020)) that allows, at least on a conceptual level, to engage with what is to come without a kind of melodrama of ideas under the rubric of The Future:

> Futurity cannot be delineated but only lived, in serial presents attesting always unpredictably to struggle, collaboration, and expression. The

Future, to the contrary, brandishing the shackle of its definite article, is always described from a parochial present and is always a funhouse mirror reflecting a parochial present back to itself, amplifying its desires and fears, confirming its prejudices, reassuring its True Believers that the Key to History is in their hands.

(Carrico cited in de Bruyn and Lütticken, 9)

While I disagree that delineations of futurity are impossible (that futurity by definition can only reside in pure lived experience), engaging with the futural outside of the abstract, generalised sweep of 'The Future' changes the discussion in a fundamental way and is crucial to the opening of temporal politics. Perhaps another way to put this is to approach the future through temporal practice, what we can call temporalising or counter-temporalising. In the investigations of this book, the futural begins through the experience of estranging the present, and entering scenes that are temporally conducive to shifts and recasting.

The cancellation of the future, as stated earlier, is really about being trapped in a present, within a narrow temporal register which absorbs pasts and futures, replete with the troublingly easy anachronisms mentioned by Fisher and Reynolds. It is about being marooned in the present, yet a present which we cannot even get full access to even though it always feels at our finger tips. The project then becomes about not decoding the present in the sense of translating complexities into its stark laws but deciphering an often bland, self-evident and impenetrable reality into its actual mysteries and heterochronic fabric. To enter into this process is to prime the futural imagination. The theoretical frameworks and practices explored by the Black Quantum Futurism collective is an example of such a process of entering into a heterochronic relation to time and social environments in which the present as such does not exist, or at any rate is a very different kind of present tense involving a weaving of past, present and future beyond imperial and capitalist management.

There is an ineluctable multiplicity of temporality both in terms of the present, and relations to the past and future, and with the temporal diversity of subjectivities, regions and races. A major aspect of the impasse around the future is the inability to think time heterochronically. Within the Western context, this stems from the legacy of the Augustinian spell of experiencing time through the supposedly clear tripartite separation of past, present and future; and compounding this, the way capitalist modernity organises time of not only production and consumption which now blur and extend to all hours of the day and night but to the time of social reproduction and the imposed time of global logistics and media environments. From this perspective, the cancellation of the future is the onset of a kind of time blindness, and the beginning of the future lies, in part, from an unbundling of the ostensible present in terms of its temporal disunity of the contemporary.

Peter Osborne's (2013) theorisation of the concept of the contemporary problematises this temporal unity and provides some defining aspects of the heterochronic specific to this conjuncture. Osborne defines the temporality of the present as somewhat distinct from modern times, and this lies in a very specific idea of the contemporary. The root of the word (contempus) signifies a bringing together of time, so not only is it a combining of forces and subject positions *in time* but also a conjoining *of different times*. This notion is 'inherently problematic but increasingly inevitable' (22) within the context of a 'growing global social interconnectedness' (26), and its problems are constructive as much as they are conceptual difficulties.

> The root idea of the contemporary as a living, existing, or occurring together 'in' time, then, requires further specification as a differential historical temporality of the present: a coming together of different but equally 'present' times, a temporal unity in disjunction, or a disjunctive unity of present times.
>
> (22)

The contemporary projects a single historical time, yet it is comprised of a diversity of different forms of temporality ('internally disjunctive' (22)); and as this single time is a matter of hypothetical projection, it is inherently fictive or speculative. It is fictional in the sense that 'it performatively projects a non-existent unity onto the disjunctive relations between coeval times' (23). The contemporary is heterochronic in this disjunctive unity, but to what extent is this experienced and understood as such beyond the level of abstract speculation? Thus it is problematic to the extent to which such disjunctive unity is disavowed in the idea of single contemporary present, and whether its speculative task is operative in existing social life. It functions 'as if there is' (23) a unity of disjunctive temporalities; however, this 'as if' may well function as a denial of its desperate condition. Yet it may also be, positively and within a utopian impulse, 'an act of the productive imagination and the establishment of a task' (23).

Whether such temporal disunity is denied or is acknowledged as a performative task, it forms a terrain of politics within existing capitalist relations and ideological investments directing the organisation of the contemporary. I assert that one way of maintaining a simplified present is through, utilising one of Fisher's fascinating terms, fields of negative hallucinations (2016, 48) which enchant us to not see parts of the world in front of us; that is, to not experience heterochronic reality. Lived time is comprised of different temporal flows which usually disappear into a present tense which edits out all that is foreign to it. Negative hallucinations are not just a blindness to particular qualities or an entity, but involve an extensive rewriting of reality to fill in the space of the elision.

> In negative hallucination, objects and entities are typically registered but not seen. If, say, someone is induced into not seeing a box lying on the floor, they will nevertheless swerve to avoid the box when they walk across the room, and what is more they will produce a rationale, a little story, explaining why they have done so.
>
> (75)

Although this notion is presented spatially, it merges into temporal hallucinations—as a kind of amnesia of the past (in which we wouldn't be aware of the time that is lost and confabulate around this gap in time), or as I am considering, of not 'seeing' the present and the way we have unseen the future. In fact, as I emphasised at the beginning of this chapter, we should resist the separation of time from space in such explorations; and instead think of negative hallucinations as a melding of time and space into atmospheres.

So then, how to contend with atmospheres in which the complexities of time disappear into an opaque present? How does one negate negative hallucinations? I do not see this as simply a process of driving away illusions and seeing with an indisputable clarity which overcomes fogged-out hallucinations. The selective blindness of negative hallucinations is actually the result of a spell which was the original sense of the word glamour—a charm of invisibility to keep the object of desire all to one's self. Therefore, the process of seeing what is not seen has aspects of breaking a spell (of a possessive relation to reality no less). Dispelling is not rationalisation but requires something like a counter-spell or arriving at the right summons. Cultural meaning is not reducible to a perfect time achieved through measurable chronology or an accurate rendering of the past, present or future into consciousness. Meaning always contends with, and is produced by, finite limits, gaps and deficiencies. I propose, following Fisher's thinking, that a first step is to be receptive to the eerie condition of the unseen present. Negative hallucinations are beguiling and yet ordinary (they make up most of what we experience as everyday life). If we cannot experience the multiplicity of temporality, then we can nevertheless observe this strange elision and sense a phantom mode that somehow registers though it has been removed from direct experience. The following chapters engage the eeriness of the present through deciphering various details, sites and material qualities through the concepts and dynamics of the ploys mentioned earlier.

We live through the real abstractions and negative hallucinations of this conjuncture: the coordinated universal time of logistic flows, news cycles, the time of consumer gratification and the present time endemic to media environments. If that is taken as the general experience of time, then temporal experience beyond this will necessarily seem disconcerting. Thus this book enters into strange times—or at least zones around which they might be located—and into suspensions where we might find some preconditions of futurity. Although Fisher did not articulate eeriness within a chronopolitics as such, he elevated a fascination with the weird and eerie from genre curiosity to conjunctural importance. The explorations I offer are based on a receptivity to disquieting atmospheres, seeking insights into how time is managed, futures relinquished, and how this control is unsettled.

Notes

1 The crux of acceleration for Noys is that 'the only way out of capitalism is to take it further, to follow its lines of flight or deterritorialization to the absolute end, to speed-up beyond the limits of production and so to rupture the limit of capital itself' (Noys 2014, 9).
2 'It is the business of the future to be dangerous; and it is among the merits of science that it equips the future for its duties.' Alfred North Whitehead, *Science and the Modern World*.

References

Auge, Marc. 2015. *The Future*. London: Verso.

Barton, Jason and Fisher, Mark. 2017. 'On Vanishing Land.' In *The Fisher-Function*, edited by Lendl Barcelos, Matt Colquhoun, Ashiya Eastwood, Kodwo Eshun, Mahan Moalemi and Geelia Ronkina. London: Egress.

Bauman, Zygmunt. 2017. *Retrotopia*. Cambridge, UK: Polity Press.

Benjamin, Walter. 1999. 'Paris, the Capital of the Nineteenth Century.' In *The Arcades Project*. Cambridge, MA: Belknap Press of Harvard University Press.

Benjamin, Walter. 2000. 'One-Way Street.' In *Selected Writings, Volume I*. Cambridge, MA: Harvard University Press.

Benjamin, Walter. 2003. *Selected Writings, Volume IV*. Cambridge, MA: Harvard University Press.

Berardi, Franco. 2011. *After the Future*. Edinburgh: AK Press.

Berardi, Franco. 2017. *Futurability*. London: Verso.

Berman, Marshall. 2009. *All That Is Solid Melts Into Air* (9th ed.). London and New York: Verso.

Bhattacharyya, Gargi. 2021. 'If You Think This Is Bad, See What Comes Next . . . Racial Capitalism and Catastrophic Business as Usual.' Lecture for the Seminar in Contemporary Marxist Theory, Kings College London, London, February 3, 2021.

Bloch, Ernst. 1996. *The Principle of Hope Vol 1*. Cambridge, MA: MIT Press.

Bloch, Ernst and Adorno, Theodor. 1988. 'Something's Missing: A Discussion between Ernst Bloch and Theodor Adorno on the Contradictions of Utopian Longing.' In *The Utopian Function of Art and Literature: Selected Essays*, edited by J. Zipes and F. Mecklenburg. Cambridge, MA: The MIT Press.

Buck-Morss, Susan. 2002. *Dreamworld and Catastrophe*. Cambridge, MA: MIT Press.

Butler, Judith. 2012. 'Can One Lead a Good Life in a Bad Life?' *RP* 176 (November/December).

Chun, Wendy Hui Kyong. 2016. *Updating to Remain the Same*. Cambridge, MA: MIT Press.

Cohen, Margaret. 1995. *Profane Illumination: Walter Benjamin and the Paris of Surrealist Revolution*. Oakland: University of California Press.

Colquhoun, Matt. 2020. *Egress: On Mourning, Melancholy and Mark Fisher*. London: Repeater Books.

Crary, Jonathan. 2013. *24/7: Late Capitalism and the Ends of Sleep*. London and New York: Verso.

Cunningham, David. 2015. 'A Marxist Heresy? Accelerationism and its Discontents.' *Radical Philosophy* 191: 29–38.

Danowski, D. and Viveiros de Castro, E. 2017. *The Ends of the World*. Malden, MA: Polity.

de Bruyn, Eric C. H. and Lütticken, Sven (eds.). 2020. *Futurity Report*. Berlin: Sternberg Press.

Duncombe, Stephen. 2019. *Dream or Nightmare: Reimagining Politics in an Age of Fantasy*. New York: OR Books.

Eshun, Kodwo. 2003. 'Further Considerations on Afrofuturism.' *The New Centennial Review* 3 (2): 287–302.

Fisher, Mark. 2009. *Capitalist Realism*. Winchester: Zero Books.

Fisher, Mark. 2013. 'Social and Psychic Revolution of Almost Inconceivable Magnitude: Popular Culture.' *e-flux Journal* #46 (June).

Fisher, Mark. 2014. *Ghosts of My Life. Writings on Depression, Hauntology and Lost Futures*. Winchester: Zero Books.

Fisher, Mark. 2016. *The Weird and Eerie*. London: Repeater Books.

Fisher, Mark. 2018. *Kpunk The Collected and Unpublished Writings of Mark Fisher*. Edited by Darren Ambrose. London: Repeater Books.

Gilbert, Jeremy. 2019. 'Acid Corbynism.' In *Corbynism from Below*, edited by Mark Perryman, 80–105. London: Lawrence & Wishart.

Graeber, David. 2012. 'Of Flying Cars and the Declining Rate of Profit.' *The Baffler* 19: 66–84.

Hertz, Garnet and Parikka, Jussi. 2012. 'Zombie Media: Circuit Bending Media Archaeology into an Art Method.' *Leonardo* 45 (5) (October).

Jameson, Fredric. 2005. 'Progress versus Utopia or Can We Imagine the Future?' In *Archaeologies of the Future: The Desire Called Utopia and Other Science Fiction*, 281–295. London: Verso.

Jameson, Fredric. 2020. *The Benjamin Files*. London: Verso.

Klinke, Ian. 2013. 'Chronopolitics: A Conceptual Matrix.' *Progress in Human Geography* 37 (5): 673–690.

Koselleck, Reinhart. 2004. *Futures Past*. New York: Columbia University Press.

Löwy, Michael. 2009. 'Critical Irrealism.' *Actuel Marx* 45 (1): 52–65.

Massey, Doreen. 2005. *For Space*. London, UK: Sage Publications.

Nowotny, Helga. 2005. *Time: The Modern and Postmodern Experience*. Cambridge: Polity Press.

Noys, Benjamin. 2014. *Malign Velocities: Accelerationism and Capitalism*. Winchester: Zero Books.

Osborne, Peter. 2011. 'Expecting the Unexpected: Beyond the "Horizon of Expectation".' In *On Horizons: A Critical Reader in Contemporary Art*, edited by Maria Hlavajova, Simon Sheikh and Jill Winder. Utrecht, Netherlands: BAK.

Osborne, Peter. 2013. *Anywhere or Not at All*. London: Verso.

Phillips, Rasheedah. 2016. *Black Quantum Futurism: Theory and Practice (Volume 1)*. Philadelphia: House of Future Sciences Books.

Rosa, Hartmut. 2013. *Social Acceleration*. New York: Columbia University Press.

Roy, Ananya. 2011. 'The Agonism of Utopia: Dialectics at a Standstill.' *Traditional Dwellings and Settlements Review* 23 (1): 15–24.

Smithson, Robert. 1996. 'A Tour of the Monuments of Passaic, New Jersey.' In *Robert Smithson: The Collected Writings*. London: University of California Press.

Sterling, Bruce. 1989. 'Slipstream.' *SF Eye* 5, July.

Tischleder, B. and Wasserman, S. (eds.). 2015. *Cultures of Obsolescence*. New York: Palgrave Macmillan.

Virilio, Paul. 2009. *Aesthetics of Disappearance*. South Pasadena: Semiotext(e).

Wark, McKenzie. 2015. *Molecular Red: Theory for the Anthropocene*. London: Verso.

Whitehead, Alfred. 1967. *Science and the Modern World*. New York: The Free Press.

Williams, Evan Calder. 2011. *Combined and Uneven Apocalypse*. Winchester: Zero Books.

1   Into logistic grey zones

[These] monuments seem to be a patent amalgam of clock, labyrinth and cargo terminal. What time was about to be told, and what even stranger cargo would have landed here?

(Ballard 2000)

Brecht, who did not want to lag behind his epoch, said it was futile for a realist to stare at workers trudging through the gates of Krupp in the morning. Once reality has migrated into abstract economic functions, it can no longer be read in human faces.

(Schwarz 2005, 92)

The examination of impasses of the future and a search for ways of activating temporal political imaginations lead us into logistic landscapes. In an exploration of low-density culture, we enter utilitarian logistic parks. The blandness, technicity and apolitical tone of these spaces will be a preoccupation in this chapter, and function as recurring entry points to examine issues around the future—prototypes of capitalist techno-futures, zones of futurelessness or spaces conducive to temporal anomalies. To investigate these sites is bound up in unseeing them—to defuse their negative hallucinations and simple present tenses wrapped up in ahistorical functionality, and instead, detect glimmers of much larger, stranger forces. Ultimately, the task might be to glimpse 'what organises history but is unrepresentable within it' (Jameson 1995, 75). Logistical zones are key sites of maintaining contemporary life, yet these spaces are certainly not given such importance. A metabolism of social life occurs here—the circulation of food, clothing, communication, psychic stimulation, energy and waste matter. This discrepancy between importance and insignificance is what we are here to explore, along with other related rifts. The eeriness of these spaces lies in dynamics around legibility and invisibility. These sites are in certain ways merely emblems of planetary-scale assemblages (usually reduced to global

DOI: 10.4324/9781315548944-2

supply chains)—a tiny tip of an utterly immense system extending out on so many different levels. Their reality lies not in what is in front of you but in so many other spaces, systems and most of all, in their organisation of time. Taking inspiration from land artist Robert Smithson's explorations of industrial and logistical sites, the aim is to find in these vast but relatively temporary constructions other temporalities—infinitesimal moments or drastic time frames (geological, cosmic), and disturbances in the usual coordinates of reality. As the above quote from JG Ballard encapsulates, Smithson investigated intersections between capitalist modernity, geological time and cultural meaning, and brought us to see these sites as 'monuments' in a sphere exceeding functionalism and economic expropriations.

This chapter, following a stage-setting of key terms and conceptual framing, consists of a series of vignettes exploring spatial–temporal composition of logistical sites. It works through some of the terms of Frederic Jameson's cognitive mapping but then takes this mapping in an eerie direction. While encompassing concrete details, the task is not to realistically reflect these spaces, but rather, to work from a border between a here-and-now real and a stratum of abstractions, uncertainties and imaginaries with the aim of exploring disquieting atmospheres that erase distinctions between these. In these investigations, I detail some of their concrete qualities and socio-economic circumstances and how these generate certain atmospheres. The tactic is to begin with clear, straightforward descriptions, and through a slipstream movement described in the introduction, extend towards gaps or instances in which the presumptions of capitalist space-time wears thin, appears implausible for all its here-and-now incontrovertibility. The chapter sounds out the greyness of these sites—probing these functional spaces in different ways, seeing what can be learned, how their qualities can lapse into eeriness, and then drain away any fascination and return to their purported functions. Before establishing what is meant by logistics and how I will explore these sites, consider an initial example.

The Corby hallucination

Located in the Midlands (UK), Corby has been redeveloped from post-industrial decline (a former location of the steel industry) into a logistics hub. The town (a post-war New Town, largely suburban in layout and housing stock) is dwarfed by large logistic areas and industrial estates. These are comprised of campuses of immense warehouses, constructed in the past 20 years and parts of it within the last few years or still under construction. These zones sit outside more familiar spaces: urban or suburban residential spaces, industrial or agricultural areas, or institutional spaces (hospitals, universities, military bases); they are also outside of more familiar logistical areas such as train stations, freight yards and airports. They are closest to harbour facilities: dockland warehouses without a dock and without a city. In a background world parallel to the everyday life of consumers and residents, these sites are not built to be experienced or even really to be seen closely except for those within the logistics sector. Using coinage like logistics hub or redevelopment masks or underplays what is really occurring here. This is an environment that has been sculpted by forces—unmistakable in ways and mysterious in others, manifestations of abstract powers both extensive and intensive—which acclimates those within these landscapes and beyond. As the above quotation by Roberto Schwarz indicates, this is not just a matter of workers, or large warehouses and infrastructures, but an alteration of reality.

Such a reality migration has been ongoing for several centuries, but we don't feel a strong weight of history here; and despite new constructions, Corby does not appear like a gateway to the future either. Is this what a futureless and amnestic environment looks like? What are ways to attune to its time in a zone where space and flows dominate? It is even hard to get any kind of time signature here at all, beyond its evident 24/7 logistical impulse. The space, too, can be disorienting due to its abstract placement—economic and infrastructural factors decide the location and the particular arrangement and shape. Other than a proximity to a motorway, these are not discernible. Logistical Corby makes more sense from network diagrams, spreadsheets and from the air or in satellite images of regions; in fact, they are built from and for these vantages and normally unseen gazes. They are also generated through adjacent conditions which are transferred over, for example, the Midlands Logistics Park promotes the low gross weekly pay average and the number of unemployed people in Corby as an attractive demographic of the site (Midlands Logistics Park 2021). These logistic areas begin as one moves out of the town centre past the Tesco Superstore into a cluster of 'older' (from 10 to 20 years past) giant warehouses (CEVA Logistics, iForce, Iron Mountain). Further out one finds recently constructed subdivision 'villages,' and then into the newly built logistic park (John Lewis distribution, Eddie Stobart, Europa Worldwide) near the Cazoo Preparation Centre Corby (an online used car company, with a 'preparation, processing and imaging facility') which is comprised of mainly parking lots that stretch over a kilometre.

These spaces are partly illegible because we lack a language for them—we see them all the time but tend to ignore them like household fixtures. Politically, they are outside most of our terms of reference and mythologies—lacking the associations of the factory; the metropolitan centre with its institutions, cultural sites, locations of pivotal historical moments; and also distinct from the suburbs with their increasingly decisive political base and post-war cultural narratives. These are spaces of recent infrastructure that drive a new political ordering (Cowen 2012), and are culturally under-coded. They are ubiquitous, crucial sites of contemporary capitalism yet largely unknown. They lie within the present's idea of the future—cutting edge of digital infrastructure, new formations of commerce and sociality—yet in a vague, dematerialised 'cloud' imaginary of virtual entities, and thus largely erased.

Rudy Giuliani's infamous press conference, following the 2020 American presidential election, held in the parking lot of Four Seasons Total Landscaping (on the outskirts of Philadelphia near the I95) being a notable exception of media attention to such zones. In fact, it was seen as outrageous precisely because of the combination of Giuliani's crazed presence in such an underwhelming site completely off the normal political map. The location was deliberate and was not supposed to be in the Four Seasons Hotel in central Philadelphia as was assumed by many media commentators. It was actually chosen to avoid protest (from activists based in the metropolitan core) and to situate the event closer to the areas where Trump's supporters live (Burns 2020). Some of the few examples of cultural sites located in the logistics penumbra include theme parks (such as Drayton Manor in the Midlands), 'mega churches' (primarily in the US but are appearing in the UK) and Prince's Paisley Park which is coming to be seen as a Graceland for the twenty-first century. It is located in Chanhassen (an exurb of Minneapolis), near a highway exit and beside self-storage warehouses. The largely windowless mansion of this enigmatic musical legend is comprised of a big box utility structure originally designed as a storage facility and recording complex.

'Our present as fundamentally a *time* of *logistic space*' (Cowen 2012, 5)

A conventional definition of logistics is an activity that organises the distribution of goods to customers. However, logistics goes well beyond mere shipping into a 'social and spatial assembly' (200). These spaces are key sites in supply systems, yet the activity is more complex and extensive. Logistics has come to define contemporary capitalism ('supply chain capitalism' Tsing 2009), and is an integral aspect of a new geopolitical imaginary (Cowen 2012) in which states and borders are configured differently than the Westphalian sovereignty of territorial states. Current logistics is comprised of emergent interactions between trade, security and military enacted in 'a new map of the world' (1). Logistical sites and practices function as a fundamental organisation of life and as a mechanism of control. Capital has reorganised in a logistical manner, supposedly overcoming crises of accumulation in an acceleration of commodity flows, decreased turnover times, and in the exploitation of labour markets. This logistics revolution is associated with terms like lean manufacturing, flexibility, pull production and just-in-time inventory systems; but it goes beyond what we think of as a more limited economic activity and conveyance from production site to consumption. To begin with, commodities today are manufactured across logistics space rather than in a singular place, as such, '[l]ogistics relies heavily on complex calibrations of multiple locations' (Cowen 205) to the point where it is misleading to see a single site in isolation. Through the twentieth century, the purview of logistics expanded. 'The military art of moving stuff gradually became not only the "umbrella science" of business management but, in Nigel Thrift's words, "perhaps the central discipline of the contemporary world"' (4). But the rise and amplification of logistics extend into even more fundamental relations to life, with major epistemological and ontological presumptions which are relentlessly enforced on populations. The 'logistical gaze' (Harney 2018; Rossiter 2019) is a way of apprehending life through the logic of the organisation of circulation. It requires far-reaching access, tracking, measuring and calculation, and these kinds of logistical relations enter almost all major institutions (education, health, etc.) and shape a great deal of everyday experience.

My intention is to examine some of the most conventional logistical sites—in their concrete, material particularity—but through an analysis that embraces a very extensive understanding of the concept, especially as it is elucidated in Stefano Harney and Fred Moten's remarkable writing on contemporary social life and political thought (2013, 2021). From its founding moment in the Atlantic slave trade, logistics seeks to containerise and put into 'the hold' (2013, 87) as much of life as possible—even if it can never really control it. In this way, logistics is at the very centre of capitalist modernity. It is the modality that drives imperialism and capital's appropriation of value—its tapping of vitality—through relentless rationalising, individualising and dematerialising. As such, it requires us 'to do without thinking, to feel without emotion, to move without friction, to adapt without question, to translate without pause, to desire without purpose, to connect without interruption' (87). Harney and Moten stress the pivotal move from the strategic subject to the logistical object. Logistics displaces strategy in both war and business. 'Traditionally strategy led and logistics followed. Battle plans dictated supply lines. No more' (88). Logistics is no longer the means of supplying the army, rather, circulation is the war. Within logistical capitalism, this is then generalised into a condition of everyday life. Accordingly, rather than acting upon subjects, the logistical order works through the idea of converting human subjects to objects within its circulations, or at least into the halfway house of the automatic subject. '[A]s Marina Vishmidt reminds us, the automatic subject of capital that human capital seeks to emulate, is a hollow subject, and a subject dedicated to hollowing itself' (90).

A not insignificant dimension of this expansion of logistics that I will be exploring is its blandness—the logistical void of tedious technical details, identical units (containers, rows of servers, pallets), office park aesthetics, etc. That is, I am detailing materiality within sites of profound dematerialisation. Logistic sites exhibit a blank aesthetics (broad unadorned surfaces, simple rectangular forms, dull colouring, etc.). The bodies, land and constructions of these sites are within a hyper-abstract and instrumental modality that seems to render all matter as generic as possible with the objective of producing a 'space of infinite equivalence' (Jameson 410). This is an aesthetic dimension of a carefully advanced neutrality, wherein land grabs, alterations of borders and the militarisation of space are presented as apolitical, or more likely, antipolitical 'technicity' (Cowen 4). The supposed neutrality of the mere efficiency of shipping is within 'the antipolitical assemblage of logistics' (4) which conceals contestation and the melding of civilian and military functions.

A desire called cognitive mapping

How to engage these spaces and in what mode of exploration and analysis? Jameson's concept of cognitive mapping—in its drive to connect everyday experience to vast forces—provides some key parameters and a starting point, especially in its basic premise that the most formative elements of everyday life are absent yet there is an enforcement of a larger systemic control stemming from these missing forces. Cognitive mapping begins from the feeling of disorientation arising from rifts between experience and vast, complex socio-economic forces. When swathes of reality have transferred into various kinds of abstractions, perceptual experience loses its baring. There is a continual perplexity in not being able to place our everyday situations within larger forces (the totality of class relations, capitalist power, the real conditions of one's existence), and even a sense that we lack access to large sections of our own social reality. This disorientation is usually euphemised, denied or looped back to us as continuity based on repetitiveness and familiarity. In a way, to even experience such disorientation and sense such pervasive absences is a considerable achievement and opens the way for a practice of orientation—cognitive mapping. Jameson advanced the idea of cognitive mapping not as a method but as 'a call' for such mapping process to be developed, which would 'enable a situational representation on the part of the individual subject to that vaster and properly unrepresentable totality which is the ensemble of society's structures as a whole' (Jameson 1991, 51).

Toscano and Kinkle (2014) revisited the practice of cognitive mapping, locating it within the context and debates of the first decades of the twenty-first century. They encapsulate it as 'a practice of orientation that would be able to connect the abstractions of capital to the sense-data of everyday perception.' (18) In their entry into the 'desire called cognitive mapping,' (Jameson 1995, 3) Tascano and Kinkle stress that it is not a method but rather a problem—'the problem of visualising or narrating capitalism today' (Tascano and Kinkle, 32). This contemporary problem has its roots in colonisation, and specifically, the imposition of a world view that renders actual conditions invisible. Because 'a kind of political and economic invisibility undergirds a representational order' (21) which aesthetics serves to regulate and maintain, aesthetics might also serve as a practice to interrogate the process.

Jameson developed the concept by 'transcoding' mapping practices from urban planner Kevin Lynch who looked at how effective planning enables residents to make the city legible in their own terms and experience. 'Imageability' is needed if people are not to be alienated from their urban environments. Jameson combines aspects of this with the task of placing ourselves within complex social systems and the totality of class relations. The objective is then a kind of 'disalienation' through creating analogous activities of Lynch's city dwellers who attempt a reinhabitation of place through 'construction or reconstruction of an articulated ensemble which can be retained in memory, and which the individual subject can map and remap along the moments of mobile, alternative trajectories' (Jameson 1991, 51).

This process of disalienation is one of the main reference points for my exploration of logistic spaces. However, although my engagement with these sites is within a cognitive mapping ethos, I see it is necessary to expand the practice into what we can provisionally call weird mapping. To begin with, to move from a condition of disorientation to orientation ought to be problematised, and to acknowledge that these states are not necessarily opposites. Orientation does not mean a cut-and-dry analysis delivering us to a stark and sober rendering of the capital's world. Perhaps disorientation is more than just as the starting point, but as a kind of affective condition to work with and through. Types or even genres of disorientation, in effect, orient different kinds of practice of cognitive mapping. We must first be attuned to disorientation, an essential staging for orientation. We need to disassociate many given dubious coordinates, and in effect, trigger our own tactical disorientation which is the precondition for such mapping, and possibly, overturning the logistical gaze. Cognitive mapping is certainly not a mirroring within a representational drive. Disturbances (jamming, counter-intelligence, tactical distortions, etc.) need to occur in order to fathom what is otherwise invisible. How to activate mapping in logistical zones where the force of the here and now is so incredibly strong? Indeed logistics, in the expanded sense I am exploring, is one of the critical transmission points of the time signature of contemporary reality.

When I assert weird mapping as a necessary part of the process, I am specifically working with an emphasis on exploring temporal qualities. If one of the major sources of disorientation lies in the containment of the here and now (the imposition of a particular temporality), then dislodging this temporal constriction is critical in surveying these zones. The coordinates must be skewed in order for the environment to become intelligible, and in terms of time, this means examining assumptions in duration, relations to the past and future. There is certainly an historical aspect of Jamesonian cognitive mapping (within his three stages of geopolitical development), and a critical commentary on the politics of time, yet the emphasis is on the problem of spatial representation and space in general. Even though Jameson saw the postmodern period as 'eschew[ing] temporality for space' (1991, 134), and lamented the passing of 'a temporality-obsessed age' (134) as seen in Faulker's modernist writing where perceptual experience is paramount for a reckoning with temporal-material conditions; nevertheless, Jamesonian cognitive mapping is my view overwhelmingly spatial. This begins with the fundamentally spatial metaphor of mapping, and extends to his writing on architectural spaces, analysis of how space is filmed in movies, mediations on the relation of interior to exterior and so on. All this leaves 'spatial issues as its fundamental organizing concern' (51), and consequently leaves open the intriguing question of what might a time-biased cognitive mapping look like.

Jameson's ideas around cognitive mapping are, given its literally impossible objectives (depicting the totality of social space), necessarily creative and open. Starting with his very idea of what mapping could mean: 'once you knew what "cognitive mapping" was driving at, you were to dismiss all figures of maps and mapping from your mind and try to imagine something else' (Jameson 1991, 409). Cognitive mapping for Jameson is certainly not a literal plotting of charts, nor is it the formulation of simplistic socialist narratives to provide orientation; rather, it encompasses tactics such as inscribing a narrative of defeat as a way of causing 'the whole architectonic of postmodern global space to rise up in ghostly profile behind itself, as some ultimate dialectical barrier or invisible limit' (1991, 414). In this light, perhaps my attempts at mapping are actually quite true to this side of the Jamesonian project, with this 'imagine something else' imperative being the key—a call for resourcefulness and inventiveness. This 'something else' for me lies in the study of the spatial–temporal melding of logistic sites and their strange atmospheres.

Warehouse fundamental

This writing is in part derived from field trips to these under-imagined logistic sites between 2014 and 2020 primarily in the Midlands 'Golden Triangle' between Birmingham, Leister and Milton Keynes, and bound by the M1, M6 and M42 motorways. From here 90% of the UK population can be reached within four hours drive and where about 40–50% of the warehouses in the UK are located (Russell Schiller). 'There is an estimated 150 million square feet of warehouse space in the Midlands—more than in Greater London, Scotland and Wales combined' (Purvis n.d.). These are mostly located in the urban periphery (on the edge of cities or sometimes as islands bordered by the rural) and consist of distribution centres, Amazon 'Fulfilment Centres', office parks, big box retail and transportation infrastructure. They are comprised of primarily newly constructed buildings: two–three-storey office blocks, occasional express hotels and most notably, very large warehouses. One may never set foot inside these spaces; however, a statistically abstract citizen has a parallel volume in their interiors. According to property company Savills (Laing 2021), the UK is an 'under-warehoused country' with a warehousing stock of about 7.6 square feet of space per person compared to the US at 39 square feet per person. Warehouse real estate has been increasing in value globally even as GDP growth dwindled after the financial crisis, and in the UK has been steadily gaining in value even before the Covid-19 pandemic. The experience of the pandemic has, at this time of writing, dramatically intensified the value and primacy of logistics though not really changed its under-coded status.

The buildings are massive, horizontal, uniform, rectilinear, opaque (windowless) and with tidy landscaping formed of low maintenance, drought-tolerant plantings attractive in any season. These warehouses are almost always steel-framed, with laser flat concrete floors and metal sidings in generally neutral colours but a few (in consumer storage facilities) use more intense colours. The enticing visual aspect of these zones is the scale of the buildings. The dimensions are meaningless within typical domestic reference points: some of them are close to half a million square feet and stretch horizontally almost half a kilometre long. The architectural profession thus far has had only a tangential relation to these structures—this is terminal architecture in all senses (see Martin Pawley 1998). The scale is monumental although their appearance is otherwise uninteresting. They are extreme like that—immense and nondescript monuments to capitalism's organisational power. The horizontal axis is everything. If the vertical skyscraper is the hallmark of the metropolis, then the great horizontal box looming on the edge of the motorway is the post-metropolitan quintessence. This is a landscape of big boxes, and it is the usually unseen and asymmetrical complement to the consumer's unboxing moment.[1] For all the massive size and volume of freight, it is a relatively provisional-built environment. A warehouse can be built within 41 days (waredock.com), most of the structures in logistic parks in the UK have been constructed within the last 10–20 years and are designed to be replaced after 30 years.

The structures are mute from the outside and the sonic landscape around them is disturbingly quiet. There is sound nevertheless, consisting mainly of traffic noise—trucks on the local roads and the omnipresent nearby motorway. The sound of high-speed, multilane traffic is almost always present around these spaces, just out of sight but audible, ceaseless like an economic wind, neoliberal tinnitus. Listening further and further into that sound, it seems to come from everywhere, yet the sound moves further into itself.

Maximum logistics

Do these spaces appear instead of the future? They are both thresholds of *a* future and areas where time collapses. Past, present and future are compressed into an actual—the time of global circulations, capitalist metabolism, the 24/7 supply chains, the imposition of a homogenous 'Zulu time.' Have we come here to feel as modern as we can, supermodern? Rimbaud's command—'One must be absolutely modern' (Rimbaud 1966, 209)—was a warning and a farewell in a future tense imperative. In lieu of radiance and actual emancipation, there is the resignation of being fully modern, fully automated, etc.

The real reason to come here is for a particular encounter with the present—such as it is. Logistic zones are a crux of an inevitability, a spatial–temporal manifestation of capitalist realism. Rather than feeling it pervasively, in the saturation of our daily lives as distant subjects, in the working fiction of privacy and individual experience—why not make it into a critical ritual, a scene of assumption into the true heart of the twenty-first century in its merciless functionalism. Beyond whatever practical purpose, these immense blank forms are part of the inevitability complex. We can speak of domination in many different terms, but arid temporality is particularly effective. José Muñoz (2009) understood it this way, in which he sought affective powers against the 'the devastating logic of the world of the here and now, a notion of nothing existing outside the sphere of the current moment' (12). The structures are vertiginous despite their sheer horizontality. They are emerging out of the depths of the Mariana Trench though landlocked in the Midlands Logistics Park in Corby, Northamptonshire, discharging a flood of microplastics and exasperation.

Incontrovertible landscapes

JG Ballard, whose fascination in the London area lay in the area around Heathrow and decidedly not in the historic centre, spoke of the inversion of airports having cities, rather than cities being served by their airports. 'The city'—the twentieth-century metropolis, the historic core, the part that looks like urbanity—as out there, a namesake and alibi for these facilities, a product long ago superseded by its by-product, the metropolitan city as a diskette 'save' icon in a time of cloud memory. Ballard formulated this view in the 1970s and 80s back when it felt more like near-future science fiction and a provocation. There is a persistent denial of this condition even as it has nevertheless become increasingly incontrovertible. These are walks through such denied realities, which have extended in so many different directions and levels. It is hardly only the centrality of logistics which is being denied. These spaces still do not feel culturally sanctioned or even intelligible in spite (or because) of their banality and ubiquity—they are still a proposition even as we are living through them.

Journey to the centre of the economy

Coming here to 'see the economy'—the global flows of commodities, the enormous technical systems that shape our world—is like walking around Wall Street or Canary Warf expecting to understand investment banking, stumbling across the levers of control or seizing the power crystal that lies at the heart of the US Capitol Building. Dum, bluntly literal, desperate— but where else to go? We lack 'the virtual external point' (Toscano and Kinkle 2014, 41) which would grasp this, and so in lieu of a better plan, come here. How does one see such calibration, multiplicity, that is, without an enormous research team, an army of data scientists, an array of information gathering and analysis matching the complexity of the system? We have been instructed from birth that the economy is everything and we have gone the extra mile to complete the mission, admire the destiny. Like a TV alien from the 1970s misreading human culture and seeing Ronald McDonald as the president, presenting ourselves for the golden encounter? If reality has migrated, extended, calibrated—what can tangibly be seen and experienced? Surely there are a few other options than contributing to a conspiracy theory on social media platforms.

But we (as in those bound by a weird fascination) do not come here to locate the source of power in an increasingly complex global context per se; rather, we are walking directly into a situation that further activates an incoherence between experience and abstraction that characterises capitalist modernism. That is the actual spectacle, and the task is then to figure out how to gage it—tracing out the basic disorientation, following a compulsion, placing ourselves in the tableau; or maybe this is just the only suitable place left to go and reckon. It is better to see these sites not as 'centres' but rather as fault lines or ley lines of contemporary capitalism. The invisible alignment of key sites, interspersed with monuments, structures and natural landforms, media corridors and organisational channels. That we are facing the society of the spectacle in this logistic park—not as mass media image but ideology made material.

As if attracted by some force within—a logistical current is a strange attractor whose presence is experienced everywhere yet is usually only detectable in the practices it (de)forms. The instinct is to get out there and trace it back to if not to the source (which is impossible) then to its local conduit, a base for a grey ceremony with its manna however meagre, nuanced or downright weird. Somewhere to go and witness and scrutinise all this, to work through a series of experiences, concepts and imaginings. There is a long line of these interrogations on the edges of the metropolis—Surrealist suburban rail journeys, Robert Smithson's 'Tour of the Monuments' with its ruins in reverse and zero panoramas, Iain Curtis' search for a phantom friend in the Interzone. Following the Ballardian path, through the suburbs and beyond, Will Self writes that 'the fiction of the 21st century . . . was there in the Isle of Grain, there in the interzones . . . there in our numbed responses to those superfluities of space and time' (Self 2009, 16). But where and what was 'there'? All those explorations associated with psychogeography and British-style deep topology were based around moving further and further into these spaces. As Iain Sinclair puts it, '[t]his wandering . . . at the edge of the city is like a strange millennial compulsion to be there and make some kind of record or response as a way of coping with the monolithic energies that are oppressing us' (Sinclair 2011). Although in many ways Sinclair's exploration of the edgelands is invariably about moving back to find buried histories and lost cities, and rarely on their contemporary and futural projections. The atmosphere of these zones, these speculative warehouses, is dominated by the futures industry where, in Kodwo Eshun's words, an 'oscillation between prediction and control is being engineered' (2003, 290).

Logistics already seen (but not yet)

There is a sense of familiarity that is beyond the ubiquity of these spaces, outside the generic qualities. Catching sight of the structures through the budding trees with the feeling that they have already been seen. Not only by everyone all the time but to see the present as something doubled, even exponentially viewed; and rather than desensitising, prepares the ground. A lingering sense of retracing something that has already happened (a ghost image from a previous time it was run, shapes burned into the monitor), that is, already happened but not necessarily in the past (akin to a simulation, a virtual version). This feeling of a fourth or fifth view is neither relegation nor advancing it to a higher level of ontological significance. My visitations to these sites and the project itself have been passed through a filter on a relatively low setting which renders everything as a partially recalled thought or a scant dream. A sense of recognition freed from diachronic, linear procession but not exactly ending in revelation. And that has been the main achievement so far—this isn't losing reality, rather its temporal doubling is eerie, a strangeness specific to the blankness of these sites, that brings us inside 'the world-knot' (Bloch 1996, 303). For Bloch, one of the crucial political tasks was to infiltrate the 'darkness of the lived moment' (12). The usual narrow confines and neglect within which routine instances occur. Utopian energies should not be exiled to far futures, but inculcated in 'this most immediate nearness' (12). The future is most often lost in these instants in the infra-ordinary before it even begins. It takes the most powerful, inventive perception to penetrate the here and now, 'the nearest near . . . the most immediate immediacy' (12). The future does not only exist in the far distance but also has to be liberated from close proximity where it will otherwise be absorbed.

Déjà vu all over again, is that the achievement? Déjà vu as political therapy, an antidote to it-cannot-be-otherwise. A conversion of familiarity into something like precognition. Place-time overlap as a rejection of the ostensible purpose and meaning. This isn't a generalisation of a cultural obsession with the recent past entering into quotidian perception, as if time itself had been subsumed by the retro impulse; rather, recurrent sensation as establishing a precondition for utopic impulses. Perhaps cumulative, where what seemed to be degraded or occluded is simply a background layer that builds in successive passes into a more expansive ground.

Is there something drastic happening to temporal modes at this historical moment, and going to these sites is to learn from it, exacerbate it? In these warehouses is an accumulation of time in such a concentration that it causes disruptions in mundane flows in the vicinity. Not in the way archives, libraries, and museums shape and store time, more like a water treatment facility or a sewage plant. This is living time which has been extracted—from all imaginable forms labour and social reproduction, satisfactions, experiences, hesitancies, anticipations and so on. Not only are they keeping time for themselves, they are doing things to it, converting it into other forms, encrusting or just annihilating it. These are time cremation centres. The smoke and ashes come out halfway around the world or right here in invisible, scentless clouds which alter metabolism, decay the hippocampus and parietal lobes. Those concerned with what is called the mental health crisis or the dementia epidemic—which is only going to get weirder from here—should look no further. This is where temporal redistribution must begin, redistribution centres reversing the flow within a repurposed logistical system for the deep life collective. The simplest way to put this: it is a necessary temporal departure or realignment. Whether you are an activist, scientist, caseworker, care worker or delivery person, you have to leave normal sequencing if you ever want to see anything beyond what is available through the usual TINA registers, finally losing your faith in the unappeasable logic of the here and now.

Atmospheres of infrastructure and the infrastructure of atmosphere

To replenish these trials in weird mapping and deepen our understanding of slips in logistical dramaturgy, let's turn to one of the most compelling aspects of Mark Fisher's cultural theory: understanding politics and ideology through an engagement with atmospheres and strange moods which are themselves driven by fundamental tensions between presence and absence. Most of the concepts he developed move through haunted, spectral, weird and eerie modes. The essence of capitalist realism, the most frequently cited of Fisher's concepts, lies in phantom qualities that have catastrophic consequences. It is about sinister yet invisible barriers which erase agency before it even exists.

Fisher saw the weird and the eerie as being related to but distinct from the uncanny. For Fisher, the Freudian lineage closes down enigmas and converts them into psychosexual concepts. It recovers their strangeness in the legibility of 'the modernist family drama' (2016, 1). Strangeness is rendered into individual, familial and civilisational concepts rather than sociocultural and political terms. At the same time, weird and eerie aspects are usually filtered out of critical studies of social forces and political power.

Pertinent to the atmospheres of logistics zones is his idea of the eerie. According to Fisher, the sensation of the eerie occurs either when there is something present when there should be nothing (failures of absence), or an eeriness when is there is nothing present when there should be something (failures of presence). 'Why is there something here when there should be nothing? Why is there nothing here when there should be something? The unseeing eyes of the dead; the bewildered eyes of an amnesiac' (12). Examples of a failure of absence would be a bird's cry or an eerie calm. The evocative sound indicates more than just the bird (a warning, foreboding, an indication of other life forms yet there only appears to be the bird and its call); the quietness is eerie because it communicates that there is actually very much going on yet none of it is perceptible by normal means. Failures of presence mainly refer to forms of abandonment, where what first appears to be normal is actually completely divested or inhabited. An example is the ship Mary Celeste which was found adrift in perfect condition, as if all the passengers had retired to their cabins yet in actual fact they had all disappeared. No matter which type of eerie, the truth of these failures is outside ordinary forms of perception and cognition. This quality can be particularly unnerving for sensibilities shaped by a time in which the credo 'there is no outside' has become the intellectual default.

The eerie is usually subsumed within questions around genre, specifically related to horror; but Fisher asserts it as a mode of perception and being, and makes a distinction that, unlike horror, the eerie is driven by a perplexing, unsettling fascination rather than fright or terror. As well, eeriness is usually marked by forms of speculation—thoughts and feelings stretch out beyond the usual patterns and confines of local disturbances. Also, the key to eeriness is a kind of creepy serenity. This puzzling or inexplicable calmness often involves a detachment from the urgencies of the everyday at the expense of pragmatic dealings.

I understand the eerie to be politically ambivalent. When exploring such mysterious qualities, they initially seem to be untameable, outside of instrumental relations. Not beyond ideology, but something it moves through or a side effect. Yet in Fisher's exploration, there is more often than not a capitalist valence to these strange airs. Capitalism generates eeriness, especially in the way it is everywhere and nowhere—a complex, global system that affects every part of our lives yet feels intangible. There is an inability to clearly isolate it, point to it, yet it emanates through everything. This can be seen in the relationship between agency and the eerie. Agency is central to the experience of the eerie—whether this is in a lack of agency, an emergent form or an altogether ulterior one—and this is closely integrated into capitalism:

> We are now in a position to answer the question of why it is important to think about the eerie. Since the eerie turns crucially on the problem of agency, it is about the forces that govern our lives and the world. It should be especially clear to those of us in a globally tele-connected

capitalist world that those forces are not fully available to our sensory apprehension. A force like capital does not exist in any substantial sense, yet it is capable of producing practically any kind of effect.

(64)

Accordingly, we can be shaped by forces when there doesn't appear to be anything there, as in failure of presence; or failures of absence in the way there are compulsions that intercede when there should be nothing. 'Capital is at every level an eerie entity: conjured out of nothing, capital nevertheless exerts more influence than any allegedly substantial entity' (11). But that is *its* eeriness, so to speak; can there be an anti-capitalist eerie? In the case of logistic spaces, is the eeriness we feel one that reinforces dominant systems or does it also undermine them? How might eeriness lead to an opening of the political imagination? Surely the eerie is conducive not only to forces that govern our world but also to disquieting zones where capitalist rationality breaks down, where its subjectivisation and interpellation go awry in an environment that disturbs and stimulates the political imagination.

Related to these questions is Fisher's idea of unworlding which occurs in strange loops when one's sense of reality, specifically an ontological ordering, completely disintegrates. His examples are Fassbinder's *World on a Wire* and Philip K. Dick's *Time Out of Joint*. In both cases, this unworlding is a tragedy, a terrifying upending of the protagonist's reality of which all they are left with is a truth tantamount to insanity. But if unworlding paralyses subjects and dislodges entire worlds, can this be a basis of a tactical weirdness? Unworlding capitalism's world—with its myriad of failures and instabilities—does not seem so unimaginable.

So how to explore some of Fisher's concepts around the eerie, and see how they might be conducive to the unworlding of logistics? Fisher mainly engages the eerie in the analysis of films and novels (with the exception of 'On Vanishing Land'), however, he notes that 'we often do encounter the sensation of the eerie "in the raw", without the need for specific forms of cultural mediation. For instance, there is no doubt that the sensation of the eerie clings to certain kinds of physical spaces and landscapes' (2016, 61). So this exploration of logistic space is such an exercise—specifically the eerie of the big box hinterlands. If we understand 'our present as fundamentally a *time* of *logistic space*' (Cowen 5), then the stakes of the logistical eerie are high.

Eerie logistics

Distribution centres are strangely quiet, that is, from the outside. Like there has a been a fire drill and everyone disappeared. Sedate when we know there is frenzy. Inside there is the driving pitch, ceaseless data-driven pressure to carry out 240–250 tasks per hour with no more than one error per 2,200 items (Alimahomed-Wilson and Reese 2020, 278), forcing employees into the 'megacycle shift' (a night shift of more than ten hours from 1.20 am to 11.50 am (ZAMA 2021)), peeing in bottles to maintain the pace; but outside, where one would imagine the full weight of supply chain capitalism, there is instead a bit of truck traffic, a few birds, some wind. A sedate covering repels interest and occludes antagonism. The nothing where there should be something. An overall sociocultural silence veils these vast forms, connected to planetary logistic chains. The feeling they exist but not discernibly. They only matter to technicians and sales teams, or people forced into temp warehouse work; and most of these want nothing more than to forget about all this greyness. Barely seen out of car or train windows on the edges of cities, lost on the periphery of the sociocultural retina. Currently, there is no popular post-industrial social imagination that could lift them to a higher level of political significance. Instead, the atmosphere is mute, an auditory blankness assimilating air-conditioning fans and the motorway into a fatalistic murmur.

Warehouses of glass

There is a surprisingly rich strand of artistic investigations into the problem of how to represent logistic spaces.[2] Without rehashing all of the different positions and strategies, let's return to a basic feature—these massive structures have no windows. In such a milieu, it is tempting to pit transparency against opacity. After all, a warehouse is not a showroom. Even big box retail—effectively warehouse as showroom—is resoundingly opaque as compared to the plate glass drama of high streets, department stores and malls. But this conjuncture, as James Bridle and others have pointed out, is defined by the interrelations between extremes of opacity and transparency. The glass has dissolved and flows through systems, economies and imaginations. The relation between light, lens and modernity is fundamental and very complex, but has something been fundamentally altered? The glass imagination, a Baudelairian reanimation of perspectival space wherein what is behind glass portals is always more interesting than through the open air, enters a new phase. The dichotomies of glass (protection and alienation, transparency and reflection, isolation and closeness) have been transubstantiated into a more general relation to technological change and ubiquitous media. Glass hasn't gone away, it is just harder to see. In the grand opening of the true time of conspiracy and spectacle, glass is everywhere. Always onward to the glass age.

One can think of other important windowless structures—panoramas or arcades, the generation of the world indoors by phantasmagoria, the windowless houses where 'the true city' is produced (Benjamin 1999, 532). In the twenty-first century, our true city emerges from these opaque structures? Of course, a major difference is that they are not for the general public. The phantasms are based here but the consumption is distributed through the windowless infrastructure with billions of screens.

However, we still must not lose sight of opacity. There may be a time of the glass warehouse, but not yet. For now, the only glass available is on a camera—theirs, ours and someone else's. In this environment, you have to bring your own luminous aperture. Hope lies in a tiny image in a dark chamber—a miniature image of a megastructure? This exaggerated asymmetry is required, part of the method. This is not to misapprehend logistic environments or position them into a fantasy. On the contrary, to see the distribution centre unaided is to misrecognise almost entirely what is before us. Taking all this at face value gets us nowhere, cognitive estrangement is a necessary starting point and unworlding is mandatory.

In the time of the saturation of the image, even the most advanced digital cameras are starting to feel obsolete. Why do cameras still need lenses and apertures? Can they not directly digitise light through intricate software and processing (no doubt arrived at through a century and a half of photographic data)? The move from camera to smartphone is perhaps just the start. To just stand in front of a warehouse and look at it—it is a large boring building, that's all. A nondescript, functional container, much like the generic version of ourselves. Same facing same. There is no glimpse of living, suffering or dreaming. Nothing to go on. Staring at a perfectly grey sky or the back of a bus seat. Take a smartphone snapshot of an area of a distribution centre. Default versus default. A nondescript photo of a nondescript space. Overcome by indifference, incapable of finding anything here, but that is it—that is what we are seeing, the stuff of these spaces and much of our lives, the logic which assembles these environments. It is intolerable, but how come? Seeing our daily reality reflected back is the last thing we seem to want. Jameson wrote that Raymond Chandler's problem was that 'his readers—ourselves—desperately needed not to see that reality' (Jameson 2005, 287). Our own defence mechanisms fight this reality, this intolerable present. But what are we defending and on whose behalf do we struggle? The sight of capitalist everyday life without filters would be unbearable, unless it is spun into espionage intrigue or True Crime documentaries. If we got it straight, it could only ever lead to one thing—boredom, whatever that is short-hand for (see the following chapter). It seems to go nowhere, unless the game is to flatten reality as far as possible. The idea is to perfect or disrupt this mirroring?

I don't have a detective story to offer and I cannot penetrate into this intolerable present either. Instead there is a strange sense that the camera's sensor and the logistic space are connected; and there is a lot in this connection other than just the military industrial complex. Looking at the image in the electronic viewfinder of a warehouse and thinking of the image sensor—small grey rectangle, minimal, military-utilitarian. The senor's hard iridescent sheen is beyond anonymous. Ultimately, it is meant to be on a drone, the tip of missile or satellite; yet also in your pocket. A dark crystalline pane with no other purpose than to capture light in the most delicate way possible. Contemplating the sensor is like channelling an unmade Joy Division album. To convert light waves into data, and wonder what remains—the anguish, the dark sentimental by-products. Being unhappy with the difference. A reckoning with what goes under the heading of inhuman, non-organic. But life flows through it, we could say— glimmers at dawn, party shots, smiles—through the inanimate crystal. Something tells me we don't get the last laugh here. Is this just some kind of humanistic encounter with its other? Presumably the sensor is scentless, one can only imagine. In any case, there is too much talk of screens and not enough of sensors. The intuition that sensors and logistics, owing to their military origins, ultimately bring us to the same place in spite of the wild juxtaposition of scale and function. But there are other forces in the meeting of sensors and logistical spaces—they both occupy 'opaque zones of nonknowledge' (Fuller and Goffey 2012, 3). Contending with these vast sociotechnical systems triggers unsettling feelings, foreboding and a genuine mystery in what could be seen as a kind of dull technological sublime. Encounters with these seams of non-knowledge should not be written off as false consciousness or reduced back to economic or technological determination.

Opaque futures (environmental power, greyness and chaos)

Are distribution centres presaging the future, and if so, what would this mean? Are they a Nowa Huta[3] for the twenty-first century, a model for how the new society will function—in its values, planning, practical functions? Here is the future, as a temporal franchise of the dominant order. Once the airport was a privileged site announcing the future; that is, a future of conquered global space, advanced security systems, software-driven environment, novel combinations of fear and banality, jet set glamour, etc. But now distribution centres (distinct from mere storage facilities in their integration into networks of global logistic circulations) may be current sites where these kinds of futures (or non-futures) are trialled. Distribution centres are exemplary for their integration into automated systems (diminishing and altering the roles of humans) and algorithmic order (such as Amazon's 'Chaotic Storage' system that features organisation without classification in a space arranged within an efficiency only comprehensible to technical systems). They are zones where logistics becomes the social rather than supporting it. A new social form, developing over centuries, is being refined within, and these tendencies are permeating through the warehouse walls and into the general atmosphere—the social warehouse. A dimension of all this is a form of opacity specific to logistic systems. This is not about the blankness of mere corrugated metal walls, this is opacity as a sociocultural logic that proliferates into a diverse range of practices. In the face of open-book lives and pledges of transparency, the future is opaque. I am not sure if a history of opacity has yet been written that would elucidate the long, probably ancient connection between power and opacity; but nevertheless, there appears to be an evolving form of opaque power that advances through techniques of evading interest. According to its fundamental qualities, by definition, such opacity appears impenetrable.

This seems like laying the foundation for a dystopia of opacity. Yet even within this direction of speculation, there are other opacities in these constructions. Like the shopping malls and arcades of previous eras, the massive Fulfilment Centres owe their 'existence to and serve the industrial order of production, while at the same time contain in themselves something unfulfilled, never to be fulfilled within the confines of capitalism' (Tiedemann 1999, 933). In a zone where vision is blocked, might there be a space where time is extended, redistributed and redefined in a logistics without commodity fetishism? Currently, these spaces function in the background of libidinal economies, for the consumption spectacle which occurs on screens and in shop windows. What if this background life was augmented? A logistics specific to a different economics—the support of needs and the facilitation of care—with the capitalist foreground dissolved by this other logistical landscape? Opacity as the end of a symbolic cult and the advent of logistical communism. Yet this all feels like overstepping the existing situation and rushing the logistics narrative into a vague, happy ending.

A component of anticipatory opacity would be an operationalised boredom, and thus broaches the topic of boredom and the future. In the later phases of his career, JG Ballard increasingly saw the future as boring. 'I would sum up my fear about the future in one word: boring' (Ballard 1984, 9). He worked both sides of this claim—that life would develop in an automated, post-metropolitan world based in tedious sites in which human purpose would be muddled (terminal spaces, perimeter roads, mediated environments, an all-consuming suburbia); and also in the modernist disappointment that nothing exciting will happen in a conformist realm in which a predictable and technocratic order would dominate. Beyond Ballard's gesturing, in what way might the future be boring? Logistic sites are commonly seen as boring, but how do they figure into the relation between futurity and boredom?

One way to see the apotheosis of boring environments, if that is in fact what we are seeing, is as a tangible aspect of the passage from symbolic to environmental power. Media theorist Mark Andrejevic (2020) analysed automated media (in predictive systems, algorithmic media platforms, smart cities), in Foucauldian terms, as part of a shift from disciplinary to environmental power. Environmental power is not exerted through symbolic means to cultivate subjects as it did in a disciplinary mode of power according to Foucault; rather it acts on reshaping environments. 'Action is brought to bear on the rules of the game rather than on the players' (Foucault in Andrejevic, 39). Such 'modulations of the "milieu"' (39) have a black box assessment of subjectivity, and work through a correlative view of social life (side-stepping motivations and causes of actions, behaviour can be monitored, predicted and then changed through altering circumstances). In more detail, disciplinary authority works through symbols and narratives in the formation of subjects. The built environment and visual markers of all kinds must be aesthetically invested to implement this power. This contrasts with an operational mode that acts on overall environments (primarily based on data capture, with the ideal of 'frameless' surveillance which disappears through ubiquity) disinterested in internal subjective processes. There is no requirement, especially in logistic sites, for the spectacle of disciplinary power. This is the main reason why logistic landscapes are not only dull but almost divested in their visuality. The monitoring here is actual not symbolic, and must be as imperceptible as possible. Such sites are necessarily aesthetically inactive (i.e. boring) because they no longer require symbolical investment. Thus their symbolically incoherent spaces are prototypical in the realm of environmental power—designed for the milieu not the interior of the subject.

Logistic areas are like a lapse of urban pretence. In an intensely mediatised life, urban and non-urban distinctions are already losing their meaning. It was evident from the way the city disappeared during Covid-19 lockdowns—all that was left was access to provisions, proximity to delivery services and a space to travel across to workplaces for those who could not do so from home. The new index of post-urbanity was the speed of delivery and quality broadband owing to a prominent position in a system or network.

Is this a lead into the full-blown dystopia where the city with its visual intrigue and pleasure centres are going to disappear into the denuded landscape of giant rectangles with blank surfaces? A truly smart city will sooner or later dispense with the whole notion of the city. 'The death of the high street' is only the beginning. Entities like public, social and even subjectivity are residual, redundant or to be eliminated entirely. The total evacuation of urbanity (Adam Greenfied in Andrejevic, 99), as well as history and politics, will surely follow. This can only leave the sci-fi tropes of bodies in vats with wires stuck into them?

Arguably, contemporary cities have become more stridently aestheticised than at any time. So how can these aesthetically divested environments be prescient? Libidinal economies, integrated into visual forms, always seem to be intensifying in capitalist societies; yet in the logistic park, there is nothing but opacity and an eerie blankness. The 'legacy city,' in a world become platform, now functions as a user interface overlay. Environmental power is divided between low-density logistic zones and high-density spaces such as cities. Capital concentration—one of the prime functions of the nineteenth- and twentieth-century city—no longer requires urbanisation as such, instead, there is the technocratic dream whereby the city becomes a physical analogue of operational platforms. In this function, 'the city' presents visual intrigue, interactivity and immersiveness as an environment for residents-cum-users to be fully activated, and thus producing vital data trails which are captured and modulated in the other blank city.

This has a certain alignment with Ballard's thinking and gives a clue to an environmental aesthetics beyond its pure expression in the opaque warehouses:

> You see people, these days, who give the impression that their minds are a complete vacuum; no dreams or hopes of any importance—even to themselves. . . . But that doesn't matter, in a sense, because the environment itself is doing the dreaming for them. The environment is the greater sensorium generating these individual hopes and ambitions, signs of the cerebral activity that has been transferred from inside the individual's skull into the larger mental space of the planetary communications landscape.
>
> (Ballard 2012, 342)

I am not suggesting that sooner or later cities will literally start to resemble distribution centres or that aesthetic investment will be a mere matter of decorative facades, providing nostalgic cover for a severe functionalism. Rather, twenty-first-century urban glitz is an environment of stimulation and data capture which is coordinated in logistic zones and operational centres. Logistic spaces prefigure grey futures in which the environment is doing this new form of dreaming (which does not seem very dreamlike in contrast to the inner mode).

But these zones have their own complexity and strange, almost geological internality which is often seen as imponderable or sinister. Matthew Fuller and Andrew Goffey's examination of greyness in *Evil Media* (2012) elucidates further aspects of the intersection of logistics, blankness and environmental power. Greyness is central to contemporary media ecologies, and its practices and techniques underlie logistical functions. The basis of Fuller and Goffey's concept of evil media is understanding an era of supposed participatory or social media in terms of underlying processes which usually fall below a threshold of perception and even repeal interest: interactions between technical systems and sociotechnical habitats 'that enable the dependencies of objects, abstractions, representations, or systems to go unnoticed' (Fuller and Goffey 2012, 13). This is connected to transferences from politics to sociotechnical conditions, and is in accord with ideas of environmental power in the way it alters social life through an array of supposedly background functions which are almost invisible, that is, until 'an environmental shift occurs' (12). The result is 'the creation of troubling, ambiguous social processes, fragile networks of susceptible activity, opaque zones of nonknowledge' (3).

This line of speculation on opacity and futurity does not conclude with an irrelevance of aesthetics, as mentioned; rather, it is an aesthetics of greyness marked by defining ambivalences identified by Fuller and Goffey: at once the stuff of fine-grained analysis yet also a vagueness where clarity is lost; an atmosphere of calm murk or indicative of an oncoming storm; engendering paranoia or an attunement to subtlety; and grey as morally ambiguous or in Paul Klee's grey point, creative—'a multivalent nucleus that oscillates between chaos and the emergence of an order' (13). What is dismissed as mere blandness or tedium is actually in close relation to tumult and creation. 'In the beginning was boredom, commonly called chaos' (Moravia Alberto in Fuller and Goffey 2012, 14).

Notes

1 Thanks to Michael Maranda for pointing out this boxing/unboxing complement.
2 Some examples include Patrick Keiller's Robinson trilogy, Lewis Baltz and Allan Sekula.
3 A socialist new town built in Poland during the Stalinist period. It is considered to be the most ambitious example of Soviet urban planning, renowned for its large parks and social engineering. Nowa Huta is reputed to be not only a realisation of Soviet ideology into bricks and mortar but also allowing 'glimpses of tomorrow's reality' (Anders Aman in Lebow 2013, 3).

References

Alimahomed-Wilson, Jake and Reese, Ellen. 2020. *The Cost of Free Shipping: Amazon in the Global Economy*. London: Pluto Press.

Andrejevic, Mark. 2020. *Automated Media*. Abingdon: Routledge.

Ballard, J. G. 1984. 'Interview with Vale and Juno.' Interview by Vivian Vale and Andrea Juno. *Re/Search*, edited by Vivian Vale and Andrea Juno, 8/9, 8–15. San Francisco: RE/Search Publications.

Ballard, J. G. 2000. 'Robert Smithson as Cargo Cultist.' In *Robert Smithson: A Collection of Writings on Robert Smithson*, edited by Brian Conley and Joe Amrhein. Brooklyn, NY: Pierogi.

Ballard, J. G. 2012. *Extreme Metaphors*. Edited by Simon Sellars and Dan O'Hara. London: Fourth Estate.

Benjamin, Walter. 1999. *The Arcades Project*. Cambridge, MA: Belknap Press of Harvard University Press.

Bloch, Ernst. 1996. *The Principle of Hope Vol 1*. Cambridge, MA: MIT Press.

Burns, Katelyn. 2020. 'The Trump Legal Team's Failed Four Seasons Press Conference, Explained.' *Vox*, November 8, 2020. Accessed May 28, 2021. www.vox.com/policy-and-politics/2020/11/8/21555022/four-seasons-landscaping-trump-giuliani-philadelphia-press-conference

Cowen, Deborah. 2012. *The Deadly Life of Logistics*. Minneapolis: University of Minnesota Press.

Eshun, Kodwo. 2003. 'Further Considerations on Afrofuturism.' *CR: The New Centennial Review* 3 (2) (Summer): 287–302

Fisher, Mark. 2016. *The Weird and Eerie*. London: Repeater Books.

Fuller, Matt and Goffey, Andy. 2012. *Evil Media*. Cambridge, MA: MIT Press.

Harney, Stefano and Moten, Fred. 2013. *The Undercommons: Fugitive Planning & Black Study*. New York: Minor Compositions.

Harney, Stefano and Moten, Fred. 2021. *All Incomplete*. New York: Minor Compositions.

Harney, Stephen, Fraportti, Mattia and Cupini, Niccolo. 2018. 'Logistics Genealogies: A Dialogue with Stefano Harney.' *Social Text*: 1–16.

Jameson, Frederic. 1991. *Postmodernism, Or, the Cultural Logic of Late Capitalism*. Durham, NC: Duke University Press.

Jameson, Frederic. 1995. *The Geopolitical Aesthetic: Cinema and Space in the World System*. Bloomington: Indiana University Press.

Jameson, Frederic. 2005. *Archaeologies of the Future: The Desire Called Utopia and Other Science Fiction*. London: Verso.

Laing, Will. 2021. 'The Warehouse Space Race.' *Savills*, March 3, 2021. Accessed May 28, 2021. www.savills.co.uk/research_articles/229130/311533-0

Lebow, Katherine. 2013. *Unfinished Utopia: Nowa Huta, Stalinism, and Polish Society*. Ithaca, NY: Cornell University Press.

Midlands Logistics Park. 2021. 'Demographics.' Accessed July 20, 2021. https://mlp.co.uk/demographics/

Muñoz, José Esteban. 2009. *Cruising Utopia: The Then and There of Queer Futurity*. New York: New York University Press.

Pawley, Martin. 1998. *Terminal Architecture*. London: Reaktion Books.

Purvis, Steve. n.d. 'Warehouse Space: A New Strategy for a New Reality.' *Warehousing Logistics International*, n.d. Accessed May 28, 2021. www.warehousin glogisticsinternational.com/warehouse-space-a-new-strategy-for-a-new-reality/

Rimbaud, Arthur. 1966. *Complete Works, Selected Letters*. Chicago: University of Chicago Press.

Rossiter, Ned. 2019. 'Uneven Distribution: An Interview with Ned Rossiter.' Interview by Kenneth Tay. Public Seminar, May 31, 2019. https://publicseminar. org/2019/05/uneven-distribution-an-interview-with-ned-rossiter/

Schwarz, Roberto. 2005. 'A Brazilian Breakthrough.' *New Left Review* 36: 91–107.

Self, Will. 2009. *Psycho Too*. London: Bloomsbury Publishing.

Sinclair, Iain. 2011. 'Iain Sinclair—Interview for London Perambulator (Hackney, Psychogeography, Walking).' Interview by Roger Smith, YouTube video, 10:42. October 22 2011. www.youtube.com/watch?v=dHiuEXMVCCA

Tiedemann, Rolf. 1999. 'Dialectics at a Standstill.' In *The Arcades Project*. Cambridge, MA: Belknap Press of Harvard University Press.

Toscano, Alberto and Kinkle, Jeff. 2014. *Cartographies of the Absolute*. Winchester: Zero Books.

Tsing, Anna. 2009. 'Supply Chains and the Human Condition.' *Rethinking Marxism: A Journal of Economics, Culture & Society* 21 (2): 148–176.

Zama. 2021. 'Building Collective Power: Struggles Against Racism and Overwork at Amazon Chicago.' *Transnational Social Strike Platform*, February 23, 2021. Accessed May 28, 2021. www.transnational-strike.info/2021/02/23/building-collec tive-power-struggles-against-racism-and-overwork-at-amazon-chicago/

2   Obsolete wastes of time

Boredom by way of alien junk
consciousness

In the previous examination of logistic sites, boredom appeared at certain points as a strangely pivotal entity; as if it was a key—however low
key, something that at first glance would never seem to open anything—in
understanding futural impasses. This chapter moves directly into the question of boredom's relation to political imaginations. Yet looking to boredom
for insights goes against the tendency to equate significance with intensity.
Cultural theory and accounts of human behaviour generally lack a place 'for
all those less vehement, vaguer, often more subtle moods that by definition
seem to preclude elaborate description' (Phillips 1992, 68). But these vague,
enigmatic qualities are precisely what make boredom not only fascinating
but also a productive area for grappling with issues around blocked imaginations. Within the aim of exploring the possibility of eeriness and banality,
boredom is inescapable.

Braiding concepts, experiences and genealogies, this chapter arrives at
a view of contemporary boredom as a remarkable kind of suspension, not
only in terms of the stalling of experience and cognitive flow but most of
all as a stalemate in the relation between novelty and obsolescence. Boredom can be seen as a lull point from which a drive towards novelty begins,
and sooner or later as this newness depletes, collapses back into affective
stasis. Spanning individual subjective experience with a larger cultural condition, this is symptomatic of an essential aspect of capitalist modernity
and a dynamic that inflects all manner of social practices that are not usually associated with boredom. Not only is boredom a convergence between
novelty and its depletion, but this chapter also considers the strange condition of how forms of boredom themselves are caught in cycles of emergence
and obsolescence (new boredoms, old and exhausted ones). In this way,
the paused temporality of boredom opens fundamental questions of value
and waste. Boredom is usually seen as one of the quintessential experiences of wasting time, so what happens when various types of boredom
are deemed as outmoded psychosocial waste? The idea explored here is

DOI: 10.4324/9781315548944-3

that contemporary boredom's intrigue and possibility begins through the absurdity of these cycles. In this way, boredom offers ways of engaging with what I am calling the problem of the here and now (the temporal manifestation of inevitability, dominance of the capitalist continual present). Boredom is experienced as stasis or even temporal paralysis, and positions us at the very centre of the affect realm of capitalism; yet from the point of the enchantment of commodity life and neoliberal virtues (optimisation of the self, perkiness as a whole way of life), is not something we should linger in. We should only arrive into boredom by accident, and leave at the first possible chance; but to do so misses a possible overture.

The reckoning I offer here—both on the level of experience and cultural significance—is that contemporary boredom's status is best seen as an affective field of ruin. Twenty-first-century boredom is asserted as an aggregated entity, a midden of accrued and half-buried attributes—earlier forms of tedium and ennui are layered over with more recent forms. I purpose, then, a certain mythical figure to rethink contemporary boredom: as a sociocultural waste allotment (on different levels), but more than this, boredom might be thought through the metaphor of 'the zone' in *Stalker* which is not only a dumping ground for alien detritus but also as a repository of materials which defy the organisation of the everyday and act as a threshold to heterochronic experience.

Aligned with this outlandish approach to such an underwhelming subject, the mode for thinking through these ideas is intuitive with an openness to the multifaceted and ambiguous aspects of boredom. This chapter foregrounds a self-reflexive relation between boredom and academic discourses. The intention is that an exploration of boredom in this way, at this time, can be a generator of thought rather than producing definitive definitions or empirically detail a particular case study. And to begin this exploration—engaging with something as supposedly insignificant as boredom at such a tumultuous political moment (the set of crises which the Covid-19 pandemic has intensified and exposed)—calls for a few words on why it matters and the stakes of boredom in terms of social imaginations. I will attempt this in response to David Graeber's writing on neoliberal forms of bureaucracy in 'Dead Zones of the Imagination' (2015):

> And like a maze, paperwork doesn't really open on anything outside itself. As a result, there just isn't very much to interpret. Clifford Geertz became famous for offering a 'thick description' of Balinese cockfights where he tried to demonstrate that, if one were able to unpack everything going on in a given match, one would be able to understand everything about Balinese society: they're conceptions of the human condition, of society, hierarchy, nature, all the fundamental passions

and dilemmas of human existence. This simply would not be possible to do with a mortgage application, no matter how dense the document itself; and even if some defiant soul set out to write such an analysis— just to prove it could be done—it would be even harder to imagine anyone else actually reading it.

(35)

In a way, Graeber himself took up this challenge in his examination of contemporary bureaucracy within his larger and often astonishing, life-long study of imagination, oppression and emancipation in a life that was devastatingly cut-short. In this particular essay, he produces some profound insights on hierarchy and the human condition wrapped up in bureaucracy; however, his approach is to find these insights not in the analysis of boredom in bureaucratic settings—with its dull modalities, negative textures and denuded psychic landscape—because that is, for him, impossible. In his view, the study of boredom (in this case, a sub-experience of bureaucracy which is his real focus) is hopeless because it is largely a vacuum. Its reality lies outside such empty experience in the brutal, largely arbitrary mechanisms of domination. Within these terms, those of us oriented to exploring this supposed emptiness (the writers and researchers engaged in the cultural analysis of what might be called boredom studies) are therefore left, whether in defiance or more likely folly, to assert that to understand some small aspects of boredom may indeed lead to insights on vast, interconnected sets of practices and concepts; maybe even understanding something significant about post-neoliberal conditions and mentality. Graeber notes that a series of very significant works of fiction (e.g. Franz Kafka, David Foster) have embraced this very task, but critical studies are far and few between because they do not know how to deal with a vacuum. Academic analysis and sensibility are best employed in 'areas of density' (34). According to Graeber, this led Foucault to situate tedious administration within a power–knowledge nexus—an area of density, with the presumption that bureaucracy 'really works' (35) in terms of organising social life, as opposed to it actually being an instrument of structural violence. This violence—especially the threat of violence in so many of these systems— has a symbolic component but it would be a mistake to look too hard for interpretive depth and social significance in these kinds of procedures. 'Bureaucratic procedure invariably means ignoring all the subtleties of real social existence and reducing everything to preconceived mechanical or statistical formulae' (46); and there is also the problem of mistakenly reading such subtleties into the tedium of administrative life.

Graeber is working within a more or less clean distinction between dry administrative functions—the titular 'Dead Zones of the Imagination'—and sites animated by vivid imagination. These divisions can be seen within larger political struggles (such as in the 1960s counter-culture, la pensée'68; as well as to a certain extent contemporary movements such as the Occupy Movement and Black Lives Matter) against systems which promulgate boring forms and destroy the imagination. The left used to be dedicated to fighting against bureaucracy and the systems of structural inequality and violence they stem from—'all power to the imagination'—but entered a phase of adapting itself to administrated life. 'The Left's current inability to formulate a critique of bureaucracy that actually speaks to its erstwhile constituents is synonymous with the decline of the Left itself.' (50) The ideas I am looking at in this chapter, which begins as a reflexive commentary on thinking boredom in this conjuncture, are ultimately about the bored imagination in all of its ambivalences—the deadened imagination and the weird, subversive energies within the zone called boredom. This would seem to be going against the grain of Graeber's assertions. He quotes the Crimethinc collective as expressing the imperative of the politics of the imagination: 'We must make our freedom by cutting holes in the fabric of this reality, by forging new realities which will, in turn, fashion us' (58). Yet I am approaching boredom as a special site, both unlikely and powerful, where the fabric of everyday reality (or at least its inner lining) is maintained; and also, in particular circumstances and practices, a realm highly conducive to shredding such fabrics. Even vast and implacable structures that appear as natural and inevitable are not free from the corrosive powers of boredom.

So how do we engage with low-density culture and social life, and what does it mean to write and think about boredom at this time, with a central focus on boredom in relation to waste and obsolescence? 'At this time' refers to this moment in history in 2021; also specific to a genealogy of the term boredom—its shifting definitions, critical assessments, intellectual legacies. 'We' is the loose collective of anyone who is at all captivated by the question of boredom, interested in affective gaps, forms of inactivity, the potentials of negative affect and reconceiving what it means to lose interest. So this writing comes at a tumultuous time—the Coronavirus pandemic (the experience of lockdown, 'self-isolation', the loss of public space, etc.), the movement for Black Lives, the time when conspiracy theory went mainstream (QAnon et al.), the impact of digital media infrastructure which is still barely understood, the catastrophe of the Anthropocene, the shake-up of economic 'globalisation', the dissolution of the European project and the implosion of the USA on many different levels. History has cracked open, yet boredom in the face of all of this? What a time to be bored. Is this 'still' a time we should be talking about the weaker emotions and cognitive blanks? Has a conjuncture dominated by lesser emotions, as

Sianne Ngai (2007) theorised, ended, and we are now back to the grand affective currents (anger, resentment, glory)? Whether boredom will be a defining affect in post-Covid-19 times is not clear, but it is hard to imagine its disappearance. Historically and practically, boredom is more of a compliment rather than an opposite to intensity and volatile situations; and more particularly, is an intrinsic part of the affective experience of political occupations, intense protest action—the long time between 'events', activist monotony, organisation tedium, etc. Boredom is in fact no stranger to perilous situations, as in the military formulation of 1% terror and 99% bored to death (see Mæland and Brunstad's *Enduring Military Boredom* 2009) or the role of boredom in terrorism and political extremism (Ursu 2016; Van Tilburg and Igou 2016).

What kinds of investigation processes does boredom call for? Beginning with Walter Benjamin's formulation, in one of the cultural theory's more compelling engagements with Boredom—'We are bored when we don't know what we are waiting for' (Benjamin 1999b, 105). How do we know this kind of unknowing and what is an appropriate critical temporality to investigate this stalled-out experience of time, that is, what temporal configuration is productive for understanding boredom which is itself a kind of temporal friction? Of course, there is also a boredom that arises preciously because we know all too well what we are waiting for, beyond being merely an expression of inattentiveness. How do we know this knowingness? Certainly, there are many other types of boredom. There is not one essential version of boredom to focus on, although that would certainly make it easier to clear away all these other boredoms and quasi-boredoms and isolate one. To do this is to miss the opportunity that its disparateness affords: a way into shifts in economies and media environments, how its ambiguities lie in the intersection of everyday life and modernity (Morgan 2003), and the articulations of this in contemporary social life. Boredom presents cryptic yet mundane ways into understanding cultural conditions and media systems, labour, institutional life, including how networked digital media is interwoven into experience. Given its vexing qualities—a phenomenon that absorbs interest and scrutiny, its shifting composition connected to context (its historical and culturally specific qualities), an emotion that is at times painful yet seems to lack substance or is even that which dissolves more worthy feelings—writing boredom is then necessarily expansive, contradictory and generative. Therefore, the approach here is to write in a way that provides an environment for this generation, with more of an aphoristic than argumentative mode of exploration. Walter Benjamin's elliptical writing on boredom (such as, in different forms, 'Convolute D' in *the Arcades*, 'The Story Teller' and his essays on Baudelaire) serves as an exemplar for boredom writing with an orientation to the production of 'images' (scenic distillations of concepts, documents and details) rather than systematic analysis. Boredom presents a challenge to forms of knowledge, and must be approached accordingly. Searching and researching boredom is not only based in examining artefacts and situations—lost keys and evidence of significant developments, and the possibility that in the twenty-first-century boredom itself might be 'only' an artefact—but also in looking for occurrences not even thought to exist, in boredoms yet to come. Also, the necessity of exploring boredom that avoids seeing subjective experience as merely the expression of larger social forces or an analysis of experience without historical material conditions—how to avoid, in Elizabeth Goodstein's words, 'both the Scylla of sociological reduction and the Charybdis of ahistorical philosophizing' (336).

Boredom is an elusive, umbrella term referring to many different notions or qualities: an emotion, affective condition, state of being, impasse, (stalled) temporal mode, discourse, an entity both objective and subjective, a blocked drive, experience (or inability to experience), an everyday 'nihilistic dynamic' (4) or 'democratized scepticism' (5), the temporal experience of abstraction (Osborne 2006, 37), a form of philosophical reflection (espoused by existentialists such as Heidegger and Kierkegaard, and contemporary philosophers Mark Kingwell (2019)), inseparable for Benjamin from a 'constellation of terms, including attention, curiosity, distraction, fascination, indifference and reverie or day-dreaming, that point towards a phenomenology of modernity as utopian longing' (Osborne 2006, 36). From a psychoanalytic perspective, it is a defence mechanism (Phillips 1992), in psychology a faltering of motivational pathways and loss of agentic capacity, in media economies a site of value extraction, and so on. Boredom is given a highly significant place within assessments modernity: a symptom of modernity itself (noted by Spacks 1995; Goodstein 2005), 'the characteristically modern sentiment' (Caillois cited in Benjamin 1999b, D4a, 2), or the 'fundamental mood' of modernity (Heidegger 1962, 228), imbricated within economic infrastructure and ideology. The politics of boredom is also notably ambivalent, as in the post-war battle *against* boredom and the contemporary struggle *for* boredom (Osborne 2006).

My tactic is to work with this plurality, to see it as a potential in terms of producing areas of crystallisation rather than the pursuit of ultimate definitions of what boredom might really name. Boredom must be seen as protean, a cypher from which many things emerge. This for me fits within a metaphoric boredom as Elizabeth Goodstein has laid out—boredom in almost any context consists of a set of concepts, images, attitudes which then affords a situation to be related to, thought of, made intelligible. The language of boredom 'figures a relationship' (11) between subjective malaise and the material transformations of culture, and thus boredom is a 'lived metaphor for the dilemmas that plague modern subjects' (11).

Historical boredom and contemporary boredom's historicity

By this point, it should go without saying, but go better with saying, that boredom is not new and has a long history; and that, as I will go on to explore, even the end of boredom is nothing new. First appearing in print in 1829 (Sutton 2017) in Catherine Gore's *Romances of Real Life* (and not by Charles Dickens as is usually cited), the term described an emotional state arising from an emergent condition—the dissolution of traditional certainties, leaving a sceptical relation to social life and one's self, producing not only a new negative feeling but a new way to feel. Yet after two centuries of boredom, not only is it not new, but it has reshaped itself on top of many past versions. Boredom in contemporary societies is not constituted by an emerging condition as much as by its own historicity—its historical fabric and familiarity conditions how it manifests yet is usually not discernible from within the experience of boredom.

> Boredom, which arose in the age of Enlightenment and was democratized in the period of industrial revolution, is a disenchanted, secularised form of human discontent. Its pervasiveness is an index of the decline of traditional understanding of temporality and desire and in particular of religious understandings of human suffering. However, since this radically individualizing experience is lived as though it pertains to the self alone, the bored subject, for whom the experience of empty meaningless time 'takes on the proportions of immorality' cannot perceive that this experience is peculiar to modernity. The historicity of boredom is visible only from a position outside the nihilistic dynamic of the experience—a position that permits reflection on the discursive regime in which this peculiar experience came to be.
>
> (Goodstein, 18)

Boredom emerged as a shadowy compliment to enlightenment values, and Goodstein's emphasis is on the discrepancy between boredom's historical constituency and the subjective experience of it. Boredom's very nature is historical within modernity but owing to its nihilistic dynamic cannot be perceived as such by bored subjects and is instead taken as a kind of ironic immorality (the Baudelairian vision of the bored mind drifting on forever, or so it can seem). This is within a humanities analysis with a consensus (largely consistent with Spacks (1995) and Benjamin's analysis) that boredom surfaced in the late eighteenth century through a contrast between the expectation of certainty (or at least a residue of this) connected to traditional social order and an emergent disorientation that eroded such certainties. Boredom named this new condition, and this novel status was integral to its meaning.

Moving into the present, there is a whole set of questions around this lived metaphor and whether the term still means anything remotely like it did during the time of the European capitals of the nineteenth century. Is this still our (the denizens of digital capitalism) boredom? Is it merely nominal— the signifier has been maintained but may or may not obfuscate what boredom is in the twenty-first century? One answer amid these questions is that, given the elapsed time, it would be hard to see contemporary boredom as being based on a response to a new condition. There certainly can be novel types of boredom that develop (the most obvious being responses to the latest technologies, as well as changes in attention faculties and time pressures), nevertheless, the basic concept of boredom is well-worn. From this, the condition we should look at is a possible reversal: in the context of the West in the twenty-first century, there is clearly no contrasting element of traditional certainty from which boredom might become discernible; however, after a prolonged period of modern tumult, has boredom become, itself, a disenchanted certainty? Contemporary boredom might be better in marking a continuity of social life—a kind of affective regularity through which, rather than creating a sceptical relation to the self and social life, boredom contributes to a baseline affective milieu (however negative or unpleasant) for the self to cohere. Has the disjunctive quality that the term first named been eroded and contorted resulting, ironically, in a sense of continuity? Boredom now signifies not a tattered traditional relation to life (in which it is no longer obvious how experience becomes meaningful, what our motivations are, within a feeling permeated by tedium and stalled time), but rather, a lost fundamental disorientation of modernity[1] (in which it is no longer obvious how experience becomes meaningful, what our motivations are, etc.). Boredom has not disappeared, it just doesn't name something new, and hasn't for a long time. At the end of the eighteenth century, the concept of boredom provided a way to engage something never really seen before. Boredom is now a term through which we can engage how disaffection has become naturalised, turned into fate.

Perhaps this 'discontinuity as continuity' formulation for understanding today's boredom has merit, and could be the premise for theorising a 'new boredom' for the twenty-first century; but it is more of a way of enacting my real point. In thinking boredom today, there is an awareness that such conjunctural attempts at redefinition, no matter how apt, will soon end up on a growing scrap heap of terms, descriptions and cultural signifiers, or otherwise relegated to the residual strata of social life—defunct moral panics and psychological epidemics, nostalgia for the golden age of modern boredom, the good old days of staring at the ceiling, the *trente glorieuses* of spacing out. Regard the chain of obsolete forms of boredom, discarded into the waste bin of history, or at least into a museum of boredom within a history written by the winners of the war of commodified inattention. Rather than adding more to the pile, attunement to boredom's entanglement in its own outmodedness leads us to a possible threshold.

Another way to express these issues around boredom's relation to emergent situations and its entry into everyday wastescapes of experience is to ask if boredom is still monstrous? And if it is, what kind of monster is boredom today? Baudelaire in his preface to *Les Fleurs du Mal* referred to boredom as a delicate monster—a horrible yet languid presence which rises amid our daily life, sabotaging activities, flattening our little notions, spreading weird dreams, etc. And in the history of concepts related to boredom, there are many other references to monstrous and demonic presences (e.g. acedia's 'noon day demon' in medieval times; the folk proverb 'idle hands are the devil's workshop'). In the twenty-first century, is boredom instantiated in the small but numerous beasts of 'stuplimity' (a combination of shock and boredom which Ngai (2007) saw as typifying the affect of late modernity) which thrive in contemporary societies? Or an objectless, assimilative force like the Borg? In my view—as I am leading up to—there has been a shift from monsters to an imperceptible, frameless presence. Boredom loses its direct animation and enters an eerie, inscrutable form that cannot be located in such an icon-driven mythology. It instead takes on a spectral force emanating from the milieu. In the suspensions between novelty and obsolescence, in the disappearances and reappearances of mild disaffection, boredom looms out of weird time itself. But I am getting ahead of myself, before exploring what could be a mythical recasting of what is called boredom and its temporal thresholds, considered some ends of boredom.

The disappearance of boredom?

The production of new analysis of boredom in the twenty-first century is not slowing down, yet there are many claims that the experience of boredom is disappearing. A thought experiment is to hold both sides of this concept in mind: The Covid-19 pandemic has raised the stakes of boredom, and we are perhaps at a threshold of a brave new world of 'exploring the unengaged mind' (Boredom Lab n.d.) in neuro-marketing, wellness, neuroscience research, clinical psychology and cultural analysis. At this moment, nevertheless, we should think of boredom as a sequence of disappearances. According to Michael Newman's (2021) drastically periodised view, we have moved from an epoch of 'the great the boredom' (which ran from the 1890s to the 1970s (112) and allowed access to a categorically different temporality as explored in Heidegger, Kracauer and Benjamin, and in so doing, functioned as an unassimilable state beyond existing economies and conceptualisations), to minor boredoms (embedded in mundane activities which allowed a lucidity to 'grasp why things are the way they are' (125) with examples such as John Cage and Andy Warhol), and finally to the total disappearance of boredom into distraction in a conjuncture driven by limitless mechanisms of capture. Boredom expands as there are pronouncements of the end of boredom, or at least announcements that something, usually the most subversive part, has been lost; and that the remaining boredom is a shadow of its former self—a shadow of a shadow. Yet boredom is growing not only by volume but in kind. 'The expanding definition of boredom in our own time means that by now one might argue that virtually every word currently written speaks of the condition in one way or another' (Spacks 1995, ix). But often are people still tangibly bored—not just distracted or caught in circular diversions?

Consider these versions of the end of boredom, especially in terms of the closing of its possibilities and power of injunction:

Walter Benjamin '[T]here is no longer any place for boredom in our lives'

Benjamin's writing on boredom is extensive yet fragmentary, expressing some of the core tensions that run through his entire work such as the division of experience between *Erfahrung* (cumulative, the conversion of life into meaning or wisdom, usually associated with non-modern tradition) and *Erlebnis* (immediate sensual reception, not connected to memory processing, constitutive of modern modes). Simplifying, in Benjamin's writing, there is a range of assertions for boredom as a space of possibility and transformation ('awakening' processes), often as a threshold concept (Osborne 2006, 42) between unconsciousness and consciousness, speaker and listener, the new and the outmoded, and even capitalism and revolutionary action. Without attempting to assess all of what Benjamin had to say on boredom (compelling accounts of this include Salzani 2009; Morgan 2003; Osborne 2006), I would like to briefly examine one aspect in which Benjamin outlines the end of boredom, or at least, one form.

'[T]here is no longer any place for boredom in our lives' (1999a, 658) Benjamin states in the short text 'The Handkerchief,' with similar ideas further developed in 'The Storyteller' (2002). Benjamin is looking at the disappearance of storytelling through the nineteenth century, and coupled with this, the end of boredom experienced as 'the apogee of mental relaxation' (2002, 149). This kind of boredom arises from monotonous but somewhat

soothing activities of traditional labour (e.g. weaving and spinning), producing a mental relaxation which is conducive to storytelling. This restful,
almost hypnotic kind of boredom is an essential part of assimilating a story.
In this 'self-forgetful' state, one is closely integrated into the experience of
listening. Through the nineteenth century, this labour/experience was disappearing, and so with it, story-telling culture and its wisdom. Without this
specific form of boredom as a precondition for the listening experience,
storytelling dies, and in its place is the 'information' of print mass media.
'The Storyteller' essay gives us the frequently quoted line, 'Boredom is the
dream bird that hatches the egg of experience . . . a rusting in the leaves
drives him away' (2002, 149). It seems that even by the mid-nineteenth
century the requisite nesting habitat was all but destroyed.

What is surprising here is that Benjamin is announcing the end of
boredom at the time when it is usually seen to begin. This lost boredom
is situated in the breakdown of *Erfahrung*—the traditional mode of lived
experience. This is certainly not Benjamin's last word on boredom, and is
not a statement of cultural decline per se but seeing this as a symptom of
larger processes of modernity. Benjamin also opens up different concepts
of boredom beyond this tranquil kind associated with the other mode of
experience *Erlebnis*.

What is deemed as obsolete

The good, restorative boredom connected with *Erfahrung* has faded away.
But what is the status of this lost boredom—is it just gone, displaced by
other feelings and notions? This is my main question working through these
examples of negative affect deemed to be obsolete; and this is consider-
ably glaring in the case of Benjamin, whose whole project is about unseating the usual views of history and temporal organisation and exploring the
redemptive energies within the discarded—reversing the Copernican notion
of a fixed past leading to the supposed fluidity moment of the present. In
Benjamin's writing, the past is active, and explorations of the energy within
the outmoded and problematising the passage from new to outmodedness
are some of the most important currents within his thought. This obsolete
boredom cannot within Benjamin's terms be simply 'historical' in the sense
of an inert artefact baring no relation to the present.

Mark Fisher 'No one is bored, everything is boring'

Mark Fisher makes the case that boredom has been externalised into a psycho-
social atmosphere and is no longer within the domain of subjective experience,
and most importantly, outside a collective response to the problem of boredom.

This idea is explored in a rejoinder to an argument made by the Institute for Precarious Consciousness in a text titled 'We Are All Very Anxious' (We are Plan C 2014) which asserts that the 'dominant reactive affect' has shifted from boredom of the Fordist era to anxiety in neoliberal time. Boredom was 'the central form of subjugation under Fordism and the source of a new oppositional politics' (Fisher 2018, 556) during the mid-twentieth century. The struggle against boredom in this period was primarily through the cultural politics of the Situationists and the punks, not by the traditional left, political parties or unions. One dimension of the rise of neoliberalism was its offer of excitement and unpredictability in the face of top-down rigidity and tedium of Fordist corporations and the Keynesian state. 'Capitalism has effectively solved the problem of boredom,' yet the price was 'perpetual anxiety' (556). 'For punk, the vacancy of boredom was a challenge, an injunction and an opportunity. If we are bored, then it is for us to produce something that will fill up the space' (557). However, capitalism seized upon this demand. 'Capitalist corporations go out of their way to invite us to interact, to generate our own content, to join the debate. There is now neither an excuse nor an opportunity to be bored' (557)—hence, no one is bored. Though Fisher sees this packaged excitement and exchange as really boredom by another means, and ultimately, boredom without a subject. The hedonic excess (endless availability of high-quality films and television, impressive gameplay, cannabis, snacks, etc.) Fisher wrote about in *Capitalist Realism* is another expression of this. This capitalisation of interaction and creativity and the infrastructure that supplies us with never-ended opportunities for fun *is* boredom—mediated through technical systems and without individual or collective agents—hence, everything is boring. In a dialogue between Fisher and Jodi Dean (2014), Dean presents the idea that a remarkable power of capitalism lies in its effectiveness (especially through digital media) of supplying us with pleasures. Our 'affective attachment to Capitalism . . . isn't dreary at all but [one] which sees capitalism as offering all sorts of novelties and pleasures, albeit guilty ones' (29). Fisher disagrees emphatically, making the case that contemporary capitalism turns on the very melding of dreariness and fun, with dire qualities continually denied (hence 'the secret sadness' (2014, 113) behind the smile of the twenty-first century as expressed by Hip Hop artists such as Drake; or in Jameson's words, the 'unhappiness that doesn't know its name' (1991, 279)). 'I don't think that the dreariness and the little nuggets of pleasure are opposed to one another—rather I think they are the same thing seen from different angles' (2014, 30).

What is deemed as obsolete

The lost boredom here is not really dreary evenings with nothing to do or being able to queue tediously without smartphone distraction (he cautions against nostalgia for 'Boredom 1.0'), but the end of self-organised responses to boredom which functioned as sites of antagonism and pleasure beyond sources of extraction for data economies and neoliberal entrepreneurism of the self.

Fisher's writing about boredom also raises the possibility of boredom existing independently of individual subjects. As if boredom is something more enduring than the subjects that host it. Boredom is usually thought of always in relation to human subjects—as if it belonged to them. The questions are usually how individuals contend with it, how they experience it, how it blocks their actions, how it triggers creativity, etc. But what about a non-anthropocentric conception of boredom, boredom itself? Have we been following the wrong protagonist?

Twenty-first-century media technologies eliminate reflective forms and radical boredom

Closely connected to Fisher's 'no one is bored, everything is boring' condition of boredom without a subject (automatic boredom) are fundamental issues in relation to networked digital technologies. Tina Kendall (2018) has synthesised assessments of how boredom has been reshaped by twenty-first-century media technologies and their function within capitalism which results in a putative end to a range of experiences comprising 'classical boredom' (82). Through these technologies, as Mark Hansen asserts, 'our (human) experience becomes increasingly conditioned and impacted by processes that we have no direct experience of, no direct mode of access to, and no potential awareness of' (in Kendall 82). This occurs through an 'emerging regime of networked media operat[ing] through new micro-temporalities, which place increasing demands on human subjects to act in the absence of the time required "to receive, reflect, and respond"' (83). Consequently, deliberative and self-reflective relations to boredom have been drastically eroded. Instead of reflective processing, 'there is a "feed-forward" circuit, in which the human subject's conscious awareness of any given situation is produced only after the fact—once their affective involvement in such circuits has already been solicited and modulated' (in Kendall 84).

A similar view is examined by Mark Kingwell (2019), who sees how boredom in these technological environments has been made invisible and almost ubiquitous. It exists now as a spectre, which is translated into experience not directly but through pre-emption. Kingwell presents what he views as the quintessential scene of contemporary boredom:

> the most vivid portrait of boredom from our own day, that all-too-familiar picture of someone, maybe even several people apparently

sitting together, all with their eyes glued to a smartphone screen and their fingers flicking, flicking, flicking. . . . These people are not in that moment bored, or at least they would likely deny being so if asked. The point is rather that this behaviour is intended to ward off any lurking boredom, to forestall the block before it has a chance to form.

(135–136)

The archetypal scene of boredom in the twenty-first century is the space and time of pre-emption, with restless activities occurring to prevent boredom from taking hold. 'Boredom is the invisible . . . spectre that nevertheless haunts the whole scene' (136). Within this schema, much of life might appear to be a negative space around boredom because boredom itself has been 'exorcised' from individual experience but nevertheless is all consuming to the social body as a threat. It has been recast as ambient, looming rather than the grey-immersive individual experience of classical boredom.

This gets at fundamental issues around the status of subjectivation and desubjectivisation in contemporary society specific to data behaviourism, algorithmic dynamics, and within larger social relations organised around the administration of data. A version of this is summed up by Antoinette Rouvroy and Thomas Berns:

Algorithmic governmentality produces no subjectification, it circumvents and avoids reflexive human subjects, feeding on infra-individual data which are meaningless on their own, to build supra-individual models of behaviours or profiles without ever involving the individual, and without ever asking them to themselves describe what they are or what they could become . . . governance without a subject, but not without a target?

(2013, X)

This can also be seen in relation to sinister configurations such as Maurizio Lazzarato's 'machinic enslavement' which 'synchronize and modulate the pre-individual and pre-verbal elements of subjectivity by causing the affects, perceptions, emotions, etc., to function like component parts' (in Rouvroy and Berns 2013, XV).

Aspects of this were building in modern societies long before the implementation of networked digital technologies, such as in novelist Robert Musil's writing in the 1920s: 'A world of qualities without a man has arisen, of experience without the person who experiences them' (2017, 158). And so what does the person have left—on the level of individual subjective experience—in a world where responsibilities, meanings and qualities have been externalised into relational flows, systems of transmission, social media *avant la lettre*?

They have nothing more or less than boredom. Qualities have migrated out of the sole domain of individuals, merged into intra- or supra-subjective relations. This is certainly not the final eradication of boredom without individual subject to host it; rather, boredom is the very consequence of such evacuation and desubjectifaction integral to modernity and intensified by twenty-first-century technologies. Boredom has always been the result of this displacement, leaving in Goodstein's words, 'experience without qualities' (2005).

What is deemed as obsolete

In this desubjectivised boredom in the context of twenty-first-century technologies, gone is 'the 'profound' variety of existential boredom that thinkers such as Kracauer and Heidegger identified as a critical response to the modern culture of acceleration and mass entertainment . . . premised on the distinctly human capacities for self-reflection and time-consciousness' (Kendall 2018, 84). For Kingwell, the age of the interface severely damages nothing less than mental health and social well-being, fundamental capacities to judge situations and relate to others, democracy and the philosophical function in culture.

Caveat

It should be pointed out that even Heidegger acknowledged in the context of early twentieth century that there was a widespread experience of being bored without conscious awareness of it ('Thus we come home quite satisfied. We cast a quick glance at the work we interrupted that evening, make a rough assessment of things and look ahead to the next day—and then it comes: I was bored after all this evening' Heidegger 1995, 109). The disappearance of the profound, privileged types of boredom examined by Mark Kingwell (2019), which restages some of the fundamental arguments for boredom found in Heidegger but grounded in socio-economic contexts of 'the interface,' is not simply a result of some overall sociocultural logic. Self-reflective and radical boredom states are not a naturally occurring part of human nature at any point in history; rather, they require careful cultivation and practices (the correct reception, time and space, aptitude, class habitus, etc.). Beyond a hard technological determinism, it is difficult to see such micro-temporalities and feedforward mechanisms as totalising contemporary experiences of boredom. If aspects of this kind of reflective boredom are on the verge of extinction, it is more likely that its material basis has been stripped away leaving it as a preserve for the ultra-elite. If boredom in the nineteenth century was a democratisation of scepticism (according to Goodstein), then a putative disappearance of boredom today is indicative of a return to aristocratic containment.

After boredom yet before the future

What is the significance of noting these declarations of the end of boredom? We can now conclude that after having considered these ends, that boredom no longer exists or it is only a phantom or retro emotion? Without a future of new affective forms—a properly new boredom—the old boredoms persist like all the other marooned cultural forms discussed by Fisher in the introduction? Beyond observing the limits of terms existing outside of their initial historical context or extending the conceptual diversity of boredom to its ends, the intention of looking at these terminations is to open a space to explore the very condition of boredom as obsolescence. By this, I do not mean that this or that boredom is simply outmoded, but that boredom is formed through an exhaustion of the new. In a way, it is always obsolete, always in a state where novel forms break down.

Restlessness and a drive to continual modification are driven by boredom—evading the doldrum of modern life through the pursuit of the new within the whirl of accelerated change—yet living within this condition also results in boredom through the tedium produced by these cycles. Boredom is in part formed by this very drive to endless novel forms and its inevitable disillusionment and stasis. The pursuit of novelty quickly gives way to the malaise of boredom as stimulation wanes, thus comprising the familiar rhythm of commodity culture observed by numerous writers and cultural critics from the Frankfurt School, the Situationist and in twenty-first-century theorists (such as Wendy Chun's *Updating to Remain the Same* (2017)). In this way, there is a fundamental link between boredom and obsolescence, and in a certain light the continual production of outmoded forms is the material expression of boredom—discarded consumer objects, including their digital counterparts (dead blogs, abandoned Instagram accounts, outmoded social media platforms, YouTube videos with no views).

My interest is not so much that boredom has outlived its conceptual pertinence—and is used now as a place-holder without us realising it is being used as such (the accusation that we are using a nineteenth- and twentieth-century concept to describe something that might be distinct or foreign from the idea of boredom). It seems like a bad idea to say boredom is dead, or even undead; rather, that boredom has a close relation to constant change, novel forms, turn-over and the corresponding trail of waste and detritus. Boredom is a product of disappearance and reappearance, a melding of residual and emergent, of the over-anticipated production of the new and the fatigue and disappointment of this novelty. That boredom itself might be just another obsolete entity puts it in a strange light—and this is where we need to put our attention rather than searching for the new boredom of the twenty-first century.

An essential aspect of boredom, which underpins Goodstein's extensive study, is that boredom has always marked a particular stalemate:

> In a time when the drives to novelty and innovation, speed and progress that have always defined modernity have become the foundation of a process of a continuously accelerating transformation, boredom haunts the Western world. It appears as both cause and effect of this universal process—both as the disaffection with the old that drives the search for change and as the malaise produced by living under a permanent speedup.
>
> (Goodstein, 1)

Goodstein is not only seeing boredom as integrated into the continual cycles of novelty and disaffection but she is also characterising it as haunting (of no less than 'the Western world'). This positions boredom within the coordinates of hauntological culture (see Derrida 2006 or Fisher 2013, 2014), and I see this haunting as composed of several different strands: Haunting in the sense of boredom as emanating out of a shadow modernity, through which the deep contradictions embedded within modern societies are expressed in its malaise. Haunted as a stunned conscience issuing from the literally rotten condition of the continual production of waste. Haunted as the presence of former ways of life which have not been entirely eradicated and continue to be felt—the junk consciousness of boredom as a receiving screen for these faint transmissions. Haunted as part of a spectral logic of media environments in which disembodied voices and a confounded temporal organisation are pervasive. Haunted as a partial loss of control of the self by strange, not entirely identifiable forces that overwhelm purposeful activities, spoil familiar pleasures, etc.

Can this stalemate ever end and what is the future of this haunting? By characterising boredom as a stalemate seems to leave us in a cul-de-sac. Let us recast the notion of stalemate slightly as a kind of suspension, not only in terms of the stalling of experience, motivation and cognitive flow but most of all as an arrested relation between novelty and its collapse. Rather than a depleted end point, the paused temporality of boredom opens fundamental questions of value and waste. The standstill of boredom within the confluence of newness and disaffection is not the end of the action but more like nearing an eerie zone that builds around an impending resolution. Can we find currents in this standstill to speculate what the end of the seemingly endless circuits novelty and outmodedness might look like (post-capitalist boredom or life beyond waste)? This standstill which comprises boredom should be seen not as an impasse but as a symptom and possible point of entry into a temporal politics focused on the problem of the continual present. If the core of boredom is a stalemate that haunts, and haunting is an interaction between absence and presence beyond conventional temporal organisation, then what is called boredom ought to be approached as a mis-apprehended heterochronic mode.

Enter a field of debris, a landscape strewn with derelict components of negative affect. Before us stands the banal emotional landscape of Western modernity comprised of these pervasive yet barely detectable sites. We are moving out into this zone, usually naturalised and invisible. We are making a passage—'we' as in the collective that wants to do this—towards the site where normal laws of reality are there, like always, only they have become overly monotonous, a place where reality is acutely boring and its laws are not broken but just mind-numbingly unreliable. This is the boredom of Andrei Tarkovsky's *Stalker* (and Arkady and Boris Strugatsky's *Road-side Picnic* novel upon which it is based on) which is a story not about an encounter with extraterrestrial beings, but rather, of the aftermath of an alien visitation. It is a narrative of aliens not invading but leaving Earth out of disinterest; however, they leave their alien waste in 'the zone.' The story is rendered with no special effects or glowing forms. It's all done on a small budget with only a decrepit warehouse, overgrown yards, shadows and darkness. In the zone are remnants and junk; yet owing to their mysteri-ous origins, this detritus is said to have extraordinary properties which are smuggled out of the zone by the 'stalkers.' The extraterrestrials got bored, left their garbage, forming a toxic site which humans then see as a medium of unknown purpose. Although the meanings and function of the zone are vague and the accounts unreliable, it ends up as a locus of an obscure promise.

This is the myth of how boredom, perhaps like life itself, came to the Earth through extraterrestrial origins. Boredom as junk consciousness left by aliens, which then becomes a cypher for many different things—a strange origin of innovation, a source of degradation and possible repara-tion, the site of the unassimilable or nothing at all. In the zone, one can find all of boredom's mysteries—the platitudes and the classics, the poison and cure, the delicate monsters, the dream birds, the weird thresholds and the ones we have yet to see. Some—aesthetic or ethical post-avant-gardists, wellness pioneers, creative gurus, affect theorists—believe in its powers, sneak in and smuggle something out, sell it on, so long as they are not irradi-ated by the tedium. Some say the alien energies have been finally depleted and the wasteland has been totally gentrified (Newman 2021, 119) so there is no moment of absent-mindedness that cannot be commodified or instru-mentalised. But the myth of boredom as alien junk consciousness is not an attempt to resume 'great boredom' or even a lucrative minor one. The zone is a place to confront what boredom as obsolescence means, that is, to find out what the aliens knew—how to leave boredom at the right moment and what the temporal composition of this moment might be. The point of the zone is to learn something about time, and boredom is the unavoidable mood that surrounds it.

Am I making the case for, along the lines of a media archelogy ethos (see Parikka 2012), boredom as outside a linear chain of historical determination? This would be a retro-futurist argument of salvaging past patterns of tedium as a way to imagine affective futures. Is there a boredom collector out there somewhere, an expert on the alterity of forgotten types of blankness? Should I channel a Blochian 'not yet discharged' dynamic where the potentialities of long past practices of boredom are not depleted but maintain a utopian current and open up a future for boredom, finally reactivated as sociality and attention economies shift? Each 'new' articulation of boredom does not erase the old one, any more than media technologies elide past ones, rather they aggregate, condition each other, repurpose, remediate, etc. I am certainly aligned to some of these ideas, however, the intention is to backup, move to a precondition of all this. The zone is not a junkyard for affective bricolage but a threshold to complex temporal relations—weird time. The challenge is not to plumb the depths of boredom so as to chart an unsuspecting pathway to the future or psychic amelioration; it is a stage to engage the confining present. Boredom is a fascinating subject, but the point is not to be bored forever. It should not be fetishised in the endless search for the truly subversive, redemptive version. The potentials of cultivating boredom, lingering in the grey layer, lie in undermining the containment of the continual present and the atmospheric inertia which allows capitalist realism. The eeriness at the epicentre of boredom is really a point at which the present tense dissolves into heterochronic possibility.

Note

1 Marshall Berman's 'tumult' in *All That Is Solid Melts into Air* (2009) is a strong example of what I am calling a fundamental disorientation that drives modern culture. Berman gives this a central place in his thinking on modernity. Tumult, meaning and creativity are linked in the continual challenge of contending with the ever-changing 'maelstrom.'

References

Benjamin, Walter. 1999a. 'The Handkerchief.' In *Selected Writings*, Vol 2. Cambridge, MA: Harvard University Press.

Benjamin, Walter. 1999b. *The Arcades Project*. Cambridge, MA: Belknap Press of Harvard University Press.

Benjamin, Walter. 2002. 'The Storyteller.' In *Selected Writings*, Vol 3. Cambridge, MA: Harvard University Press.

Berman, Marshall. 2009. *All That Is Solid Melts Into Air* (9th ed.). London and New York: Verso.

Boredom Lab. n.d. 'Boredom Lab.' *Boredom Lab*. Accessed June 1, 2021. https://boredomlab.org/

Chun, Wendy Hui Kyong. 2017. *Updating to Remain the Same*. Cambridge, MA: MIT Press.

Derrida, Jacques. 2006. *Specters of Marx: The State of the Debt, the Work of Mourning and the New International*. Abingdon: Routledge.

Fisher, Mark. 2013. '"A Social and Psychic Revolution of Almost Inconceivable Magnitude": Popular Culture's Interrupted Accelerationist Dreams.' *e-flux* 46.

Fisher, Mark. 2014. *Ghosts of My Life. Writings on Depression, Hauntology and Lost Futures*. Winchester: Zero Books.

Fisher, Mark. 2018. *Kpunk The Collected and Unpublished Writings of Mark Fisher*, edited by Darren Ambrose. London: Repeater Books.

Fisher, Mark and Dean, Jodi. 2014. 'We Can't Afford to Be Realists: A Conversation.' In *Reading Capitalist Realism*. Iowa City: University of Iowa Press.

Goodstein, Elizabeth. 2005. *Experience Without Qualities: Boredom and Modernity*. Stanford: Stanford University Press.

Graeber, David. 2015. 'Dead Zones of the Imagination: An Essay on Structural Stupidity.' in *The Utopia of Rules*. London: Melville House.

Heidegger, Martin. 1962. *Being and Time*. Translated by John Macquarrie and Edward Robinson. New York: Harper & Row.

Heidegger, Martin. 1995. *The Fundamental Concepts of Metaphysics*. Bloomington: Indiana University Press.

Jameson, Frederic. 1991. *Postmodernism, Or, the Cultural Logic of Late Capitalism*. Durham, NC: Duke University Press.

Kendall, Tina. 2018. '"#boredwithmeg": Gendered Boredom and Networked Media.' *New Formations* 93: 80–100.

Mæland, Bård and Brunstad, Paul. 2009. *Enduring Military Boredom*. Basingstoke: Palgrave Macmillan.

Mark, Kingwell. 2019. *Wish I Were Here: Boredom and the Interface*. Montreal: McGill-Queen's University Press.

Morgan, Joe. 2003. 'Benjamin and Boredom.' *Critical Quarterly* 45 (1–2) (Spring–Summer): 168–181.

Musil, Robert. 2017. *The Man Without Qualities*. London: Picador.

Newman, Michael. 2021. 'The Long and the Short of it: Boredom after the End of the Great Boredom.' In *On Boredom: Essays in Art and Writing*. London: UCL Press.

Ngai, Sianne. 2007. *Ugly Feelings*. Cambridge, MA: Harvard University Press.

Osborne, Peter. 2006. 'The Dreambird of Experience Utopia, Possibility, Boredom.' *Radical Philosophy* 137 (May/June): 36–44.

Parikka, Jussi. 2012. *What is Media Archaeology?* Cambridge: Polity Press.

Phillips, Adam. 1992. *On Kissing, Tickling, and Being Bored*. Cambridge, MA: Harvard University Press.

Rouvroy Antoinette and Berns, Thomas. 2013. 'Algorithmic Governmentality and Prospects of Emancipation.' *Réseaux* 2013/1 (177): 163–196.

Salzani, Carlo. 2009. 'The Atrophy of Experience: Walter Benjamin and Boredom.' In *Essays on Boredom and Modernity,* edited by Barbara Dalle Pezze and Carlo Salzani. Amsterdam: Rodopi.

Spacks, Patricia. 1995. *Boredom: The Literary History of a State of Mind.* Chicago: University of Chicago Press.

Sutton, Mike. 2017. 'Debunking the Roots of Boredom.' Accessed June 1, 2021. https://dysology.blogspot.com/2017/12/debunking-roots-of-boredom.html

Ursu, Alexandra Bianca. 2016. 'From Emancipated Warriors to Irrational Victims: Media Framing of Female Participation in Terrorism: Chechen Shahidkas and ISIS Women.' Master's thesis, Leiden University, Leiden, The Netherlands.

Van Tilburg, Wijnand and Igou, Eric. 2016. 'Going to political extremes in response to boredom.' *European Journal of Social Psychology,* 46: 687–699.

We are Plan C. 2014. 'We Are All Very Anxious.' *Plan C,* April 4, 2014. Accessed June 1, 2021. www.weareplanc.org/blog/we-are-all-very-anxious/

3   The enigma of Kitsault

In order to understand the arcades from the ground up, we sink them into the deepest stratum of the dream.

(Benjamin 1999, 206)

'[S]tripped away from all of the normal functional things that you connect them with . . . they become atmospheric.'

(Barton 2017, 113)

The exploration of futural preconditions brings us, finally, to the abandoned yet suspended town of Kitsault. This chapter consists of theses and thought experiments on what Kitsault might be. Beyond the name of place, it names a condition or a process. How is it constituted, what are some of its elements, and also, what else can it be? I take Kitsault's strange condition, which I will slowly unravel, as an extension of larger issues around temporality and political imaginations. To understand Kitsault is to gain insights on these larger questions. Through deciphering and learning from its atmosphere, we might glean some insights into an anomalous temporality that produces futurity. Kitsault is inherently heterochronic and explorations of it will at certain points merge the of lines of enquiry from the boredom and logistics chapters. This book was introduced as not only an exploration of eerie temporality but also, *pace* Jason Barton (2017), a search for 'the other side of the eerie, this dispassionate positive side' which has been 'edited out of the world' (90). Not an eerie that warns the curious and frightens them back within a typical morality of the horror genre and a religious metaphysics; rather, an unknown that stimulates and leads to growth within an unsettling atmosphere. Directly and indirectly, the past two chapters have been conducting this exploration—logistics' eerie as a reimagining of a notion of distribution and engaging opacity as threshold to a mysterious core within supposed technocratic functions; boredom as

DOI: 10.4324/9781315548944-4

an entry to heterochronic relations and a possible departure from novelty-obsolescence cycles. Continuing this exploration of strange atmospheres, we first approach Kitsault tentatively to avoid the habitual modes of perception embedded in an ideological common sense.

Inscrutable

Kitsault appears inscrutable, and within this condition, is somewhat reassuring because it is manifestly inexplicable. We can be sure that we don't really know what we are dealing with here. That most of the present is likewise inexplicable but seldom regarded as such may be the cause of an underlying unease within convenience—perhaps the root cause of so many mental health crises, the bad air of social media communication, the rot of afternoon culture. So we come to Kitsault to relax in its atmosphere, cordoned off in a ludic area. I can make a game of Kitsault, delve its conundrums and present its riddles for the reader to solve; but Kitsault is a warning. An abandoned place like this must bear ugly secrets. Even the intrigue of its partial ruin state should be treated warily. There is the feeling something is deeply wrong in spite of how peaceful and curious it appears. This is like a psychic dimension of the outsourcing logic of lithium extraction, exporting 'recycling materials' and farming out dirty work so destruction is displaced to some other part of the world, some other part of reality, in order that the air can be clear and people can live comfortable lives. Or like the devious game of carbon offsetting where the destruction in one place is restored in another. The peace of Kitsault is the psychic reparation for damage occurring elsewhere or in other times. Has a generalised version of this eerie displacement become a general logic of this time?

The town, if we can call it that, sits on the end of Alice Arm which is a deep-water fiord in northern British Columbia, Canada. The area is near the Nisga'a first nations territory, and a treaty between the Nisga'a and the British Columbian and Canadian governments was only signed in 1998 after more than a century of European occupation. Kitsault sits like one absurd end of the European colonisation of North American, extending from the fifteenth century to the twenty-first century; from waves of displacement, theft and war; from the Caribbean and the Atlantic coast all the way to this suspended, empty town on the Northwest edge of the continent.

Kitsault appears as inscrutable, but it can be easily explained. It is an abandoned town originally built by the U.S. mining conglomerate Phelps Dodge to house workers for a molybdenum mine. It was hastily constructed between 1978 and 1980 for $50 million (Coolidge 2008, 105), occupied for 18 months with a population of 1,200, and abandoned almost overnight due to a fall in commodity prices. The town consists or consisted of

> 100 single-family homes and duplexes, 7 apartment buildings with a total of 202 suites . . . a modern hospital and a shopping centre, restaurants, banks, a theatre and a post office. All the services were underground, including cablevision and phone lines. There was a state-of-the-art sewage treatment plant and the cleanest running water in the province. For entertainment, there was a pub, a pool, a library and two recreation centres with jacuzzis, saunas and a theatre.

> (kitsault.com)

It is difficult to select the correct tense to speak of Kitsault. Most of these buildings still exist and are essentially functional. Since its closure in 1983, it has been maintained so it has not fallen into decay like the normal fate of ghost towns or other abandoned sites. The location is remote with 165 km to the nearest town by a gravel logging road and 800 km to the closest large city by air or by sea. It appears as a comfortable suburb pulled away from its urban centre and outside the flow of time, without occupants, almost unused and unlived.

Walking down the residential streets of Kitsault, and there are only a few streets, you would see individual houses typical of those built in 1970s North America—split-level designs with wooden-siding and picture windows. This is generic suburban single-family housing from that period with some adaptations of Pacific Northwest such as cedar-siding, awnings to protect from rain on the front of the houses and covered driveways. The houses are almost new in the sense of seeing little use yet have aged a little in this new state. Despite basic maintenance, they have some paint peeling and wooden surfaces long ago stained now slivered by daylight. The lawns have been mowed with a farm tractor so they are not growing wild nor are they suburban perfect. The combined effect blends the almost new, with signs of rough maintenance and traces of decay. There is not a car in sight and the driveways have well-developed mossy patches. For a moment, it might appear like a suburban neighbourhood in Vancouver or Seattle which has been foreclosed or expropriated for a megaproject. However, something else is going on: to begin with, there are no people whatsoever and astoundingly, no automobile traffic; furthermore, the streets don't seem to go anywhere, just a single loop almost like a Mobius strip. Outside the residential area, there are a few four-storey blocks of apartments, a small shopping mall and an office block. Beyond this are forested slopes of mountains that extend in all directions except one which opens to an inlet. Looking in through the windows, some houses seem like showrooms with catalogue furnishing and no personal objects, while others are completely empty. There is no vandalism, broken glass, soiled carpets or signs of water damage.

That is the simple description, but beyond this, it is not at all certain what Kitsault is—abandoned mining town, empty model town, accidental museum of twentieth-century suburbia, cloaked digital communication infrastructure, time zone, wish image, vanishing point. What has already vanished here or what else could vanish? So much of everyday life has been eradicated, what other aspects of reality might slip away? If we stay here too long, would we also disappear? It is an exemplar of suspension, but what is its lull—the novelty-obsolescence loop, a slow motion capitalist process or lapse (a fluctuation of value, an ideological function, fashion)? In any account it is a locus of disappearance, and inevitably within the popular imagination, a site of paranormal activity. Paranoia and conspiracy are not out of place here, in an area where media systems or even an entire symbolic order can go a bit off the tracks; or refuel themselves with Kitsault being a source of content, an unproduced screenplay, or a new way of living. There are a lot of directions to go in, multiplicities, in a town where the roads don't really lead anywhere. Kitsault is mysterious yet ordinary, and the real mystery is the function of the 'yet'. Therefore, its anomalous atmosphere can act as a way to think through contemporary temporal politics, and passages from cancelled futures to possibilities of heterochronia.

The approach is to understand Kitsault as a particular extension of a pervasive state. Whatever insights formed around Kitsault can be found in other, more typical environments, or in capitalist ubiquity itself. The mysteries and peculiar nature of Kitsault are manifest—mesmeric, eerie, uncertain—and so it makes it easy for us like a training town for seeing how possibility is thwarted, how temporality is normally contained within a present (time traps), absurd patterns which are lived as unremarkable. Kitsault is a figure to explore retemporalisation and a heuristic for political imaginations. There is a disparateness in this learning approach—not just a flexibility and resourcefulness to enter complexities, contradictions and heterogeneity; but disparateness as part of the unruliness of thought. To explore lapses and suspensions is not a time for rigidity and close adherence to all the dos and don'ts of the dialectical image as Jameson has neatly laid out (2020, 226–252). Much of this chapter is just trying to see what Kitsault is and, if only for a moment, accede to its legibility beyond a natural present tense or merely tracing its retro charm back to a narrow origin. Benjamin's concepts are indeed an intellectual fuel for this exploration although certainly not a template. Kitsault is incomplete—it didn't finish what it started and is suspended, and in such a state opens it to an extensive exploration on impasses and possibility.

The last gasp becomes the first

Kitsault first appears as a hallmark of an era passing out of existence, a last gasp of something. Which era is this—the Western post-war golden age with its confidence in the future, thus Kitsault is a landscape of the cancellation of the future? Another accidental monument to the oblivious good times of the Anthropocene? Of course, this assumes that it has this passed out of existence. It is more a sense that Kitsault *should* be a figure of a terminal phase of exploitative socio-economic relations, unnegotiable 'lifestyles,' etc. As if Kitsault's stasis is a prefiguration of a mass abandonment or exodus, yet its limbo condition could well signify that this era could well go on and on, oblivious of even its own end. Kitsault's pause is politically ambivalent and highly multifaceted, and one of its facets reflects a desire for an end of an entire way of life. It is one image of an end of capitalism, a whimpering end; and it wasn't that hard to imagine after all?[1] Of course the imaginative labour of rendering it as 'the end' is incredibly difficult, and I am merely offering glimpses.

Areas of suspension allow for moving beyond the bounds of normal apprehension; so within this paused space, here is a utopian ploy. The suspension of Kitsault allows a glimpse of the exhaustion of capitalism, and even, a projection of a kind of communist Kitsault. A lapsed Kitsault after its first phase of extractivist capitalism ended in failure, would develop without private property. Its streets, houses and public amenities would then be redefined according to a radically different set of fundamental relations. Kitsault would be a world without commodities, and all those retro goods leftover from the late 1970s would simply be useful. Those who grew up under capitalism would have a range of uncanny sensations and experience a specific eeriness of seeing former commodities transformed into materialised social relations and utilities. Plunged into this new Kitsault of commonwealth could only result in one thing—boredom. Would it be unbearable for us? 'Perhaps it is too dull for the human being conditioned to life in a capitalist era, and moreover, even coercive as it pushes forth this "boredom"' (Chukhro 2020, 71). Its existing pragmatic organisation and Mobius strip form might amplify this feeling. Would this be a categorically different boredom than the one explored in the previous chapter—born not out of collapse of continual novelty driving capitalist culture but of its absence? The previous chapter looked at boredom as a putative departure from novelty cycles. In this light, 'the zone' could transfigure into this other Kitsault or function as threshold to it. Boredom, in this way, would be an inadvertent deconditioning of commodity expectations. Only those who had passed through the zone would be ready for this Kitsault.

Yet viewing Kitsault's frozen state as an entree into post-capitalist speculation—utopic Kitsault—can then just as easily oscillate into an image of an intransigence or worse. This is the existing idea of the extractivist good life and may it persist forever! Climate change won't slow us down, deep inequalities don't matter. Kitsault is the last gasp of a quaint phase of late industrial capitalism to be replaced by something far more virulent. If you think that neoliberalism was bad, wait till you see what comes next. But do not worry, Kitsault is for winners! How modest and limited Kitsault appears by twenty-first-century first world standards, still shaped in a 'jobs for life' notion of industrial labour and vestiges of social welfare. The town should be razed because it is too underdeveloped and out of touch with advanced consumer desire, network modalities and investment value. Our luxury pickup trucks will never fit in these garages, lack of bathrooms, the phone system will not handle our data, the houses are too small, too remote from Amazon services, etc.

An old-new not becoming old nor renewed (after the molybdenum rush)

Kitsault is not a ghost town; in fact, it is ' "a fully functioning community"—albeit, one devoid of inhabitants' (David Pernarowski, the mayor of a nearby town who promoted Kitsault as part of a pipeline project, cited in Dembicki 2013).

We know it is from the late 1970s and it is still in the 1970s in terms of its largely unused, specific material culture. It is not old in terms of use and wear; yet in comparison of structures and objects recently manufactured, it is obviously not new. Basic maintenance, however imperfect, produces a suspended 'new' state—neither falling into obsolescence nor being active in the present. Recalling the last chapter, Kitsault is bored with capitalist modernity. It neither comes to life as a community nor disappears. Too costly to rebuild yet too expensive to demolish. In its abandonment and creeping dereliction, it can be ruin-like. There are faded stop signs, plants growing up in the cracks in the asphalt. Yet it maintains an impression of the new with mowed lawns, functioning street lights, and all of its interior spaces and objects almost brand new except for a bit of dust and a few scuffs. In an eBay-inflected imagination, it's an NOS—New Old Stock—suburban settlement. Kitsault elevates the status of NOS into a new category of temporal ontology.

In this way, we come to Kitsault to see how the new does not quite turn into the old, in an area that confounds the management of the past, present and future. A re-education in time has become necessary—becoming intimate with temporalities that are hard to define. Kitsault provides lessons in this through its strange moments. Not a perfect world but a partially preserved one functioning as a conducive and conductive state. It might seem like a model town lost in time, yet time has found it however marginally. There is a continual interest in Kitsault in news media and online content, mostly as a curiosity piece for regional television or newspapers, or within niche interests such as in urban exploration forms and YouTube channels. Digital media is surprisingly inclined to abandonment and 'fails.' In fact, I've never been there. Most of my engagement with Kitsault is based on photos, written accounts and news stories from online sources; as well as my own experience of similar places.

For Benjamin, analysis of commodity culture ultimately lies in seeing how novelty and obsolescence are bound up in each other. When Benjamin calls us 'to recognize the monuments of the bourgeoisie as ruins even before they have crumbled' (Benjamin 1999, 13), it is not an attempt to disfigure the crowning glory of capitalism per se. Rather, the status of ruins-in-the-making is a generic medium of almost all capitalist forms. The task is then how to identify it as such. Newness is a transfixing allure which most of everyday life transpires within, but what is it really? Novelty is 'the quintessence of false consciousness, the tireless agent of which is fashion' (11). Therefore seeing through 'the new' is an imperative for Benjamin, and a corollary to denying the past as past. Kitsault's suspended new allows an insight: how a fusion of old-new, in a delayed site, is an inert state of a prime substance that animates capitalism and through which most media and urban forms emerge from. As organic life is based on carbon atoms, so Kitsault is a fundamental element in a capitalist universe. There is a trace of Kitsault inside all smartphones and social media profile pages. Devices, media content and built environments are derived from this monad.

Eco-resort, natural gas port, waste generation station and peace centre

'What do cancer technology and newspapers have in common? How about ghost towns and oil refineries? A northern B.C. mayor and China's largest bank?' (Dembicki 2013) If readers are sceptical about the way Kitsault seems to be playing so many roles, and that this 'prime substance' condition is surely exaggerated by a critical-poetic imagination, then let them be reassured that this multiplicity is also seen by its owner and backers. Kitsault is owned by Krishnan Suthanthiran who describes it as a 'pristine Shangri-La nestled in a mountain inlet' (Kitsault Resorts n.d.). In 2004, he decided to buy the town for $5.7 million in cash when he saw an ad in a newspaper while eating breakfast at McDonald's (CBC/Radio Canada 2013), and purchased it from Niho Land & Cattle (a company that 'buys towns from mining companies, usually breaks them down into lots, and sells them to people looking for a place to park a mobile home for hunting, fishing weekends' (Coolidge 2008, 104)). Suthanthiran is a businessman who made his fortune selling medical supplies and equipment for cancer treatment. Since the purchase of the site, he has floated a series of different development ideas for Kitsault including an eco-retreat, an artist's colony, a Liquid Natural Gas port, a Gandhi film festival venue and waste generator station. He imagined it as a special place to 'hold conferences, gathering scientists for forums and evening salmon-roasts on the beach' (Struck 2005). Other images make up the vision—wedding receptions, a corporate retreat, a movie set, skiing, hiking, a spa, bans on smoking and 'maybe a high-speed hydrofoil to bring tourists' (Struck 2005). He has developed these to various levels from schemes mentioned to the press or on his website, to detailed proposals such as the $30 billion bid (in a consortium of energy producers and a financing deal with the Industrial and Commercial Bank of China (Dembicki 2013)) to become a Liquid Natural Gas port for a pipeline from shale gas fields. To this date, none of these have been realised. Interestingly, the molybdenum mine has started up again, only this time it does not require Kitsault. Instead, it has its own on-site camp where workers are transported in for two-week shifts and stay in porta-cabin 'man camps.' This is indicative of the shift from developing an entire company town to house families and supporting businesses and services, to rotating in contract labour.

Despite Suthanthiran's good intentions and vague ideas for a peace centre, he has shown little interest in working closely with indigenous people who have lived in this area for millennia.

> 'I don't think he really knows what he's gotten into,' mused Edmond Wright, secretary-treasurer of the Nisga'a Lisims native government, which represents the aboriginal villages that are Kitsault's closest neighbours. 'We're really out in the boondocks here.' Besides, native officials told Suthanthiran at a recent meeting to discuss his plans, the 6,200 Nisga'a have treaty rights and a well-vetted development blueprint for the area. Over a hospitable lunch of wild salmon, the Nisga'a officials politely scolded Suthanthiran for rushing ahead without consulting them. 'You've got too much money,' Wright chided him.
>
> (Struck 2005)

A town of the non-present (heterochronic Kitsault)

There appears to be no one there and the doors to all the buildings are open. A landscape stretches between ill-fated anticipations, a short moment of habitation, maintained uninhabitation and some unknown future. In a frozen situation like this, such categories and temporal divisions are insubstantial. The future hangs in suspension between a set of different possibilities; yet the town neither comes to life nor disappears completely, and sits very much in its past. Is this the heterochronic potential I have been working towards or is still in the implacable present? Is its eeriness outside the 'frenetic standstill' (Rosa 2013, 56), can it infringe the 'present without a view' (Danowski and Viveiros de Castro 2017, 5) with strange vistas and vignettes?

One version of Kitsault's heterochronic potential lies, counter-intuitively, in engaging in the first place with the very inaccessibility of everyday life. We are contained within the present through a social misapprehension that we have full access to it, while in reality we drift within abstractions, commodity distortions, disfiguration of labour and so on. To live in a capitalist present is to be caught with an imperceptible mystery. Following Benjamin, 'we penetrate the mystery only to the degree that we recognise it in the everyday world, by virtue of a dialectical optic that perceives the everyday as impenetrable, the impenetrable as everyday' (Benjamin 1999b, 210). And as noted by Peter Osborne, '[t]he main mystery in the everyday world of modern capitalism is, of course, the commodity' (Osborne 1995, 182).

> In the increasingly common sense of Marxism (whatever the fate of Communism as a political movement), commodity fetishism replaces popular religion. With commodities, Marx writes, 'a definite social relation between men . . . assumes . . . for them, the fantastic form of a relation between things.' The life-process of society is shrouded in a 'mystical veil.' 'Magic and necromancy' abound . . . value 'transforms every product of labour into a social hieroglyphic.'
> (Marx, Capital, Volume I, pp. 126, 165, 169, 173, 167 cited in Osborne 1995, 182)

In contemporary capitalism, this mystery is not only produced by vast accumulations of commodities and the erasure of labour but also extenuated into cults of assets and financialisation, abstractions of global logistical infrastructures and flows, and within the human–non-human relations in terms of both the intensification of automated systems and to the far reaches of the Anthropocene. For Marx, the mystery of the present was ultimately a misrepresentation of labour and material conditions, and it required a decoding of these fantastic forms back to their practical and rational relations. Then we would be truly aligned with our moment of history. Surrealism worked through a different process. The task was not to demystify dreams and return to the true plain of social life; instead, it was to rewrite these visions 'in the detritus of the everyday, not merely interpreting them, but working on them, in their twofold character as symptoms of alienation (disavowal) and figures of possibility (desire)' (Osborne 1995, 99). Through various Surrealist practices, the delusions of commodification are rewritten in the obsolescent forms capitalism has jettisoned, and transforming them into signs of desire beyond the lure of the commodity. In terms of temporal organisation, Surrealist procedures sought a transformation of the quotidian present. What I am referring to as heterochronic experience would be arrived at through a recasting of social hieroglyphs not back to their true, economic reality, but into a different alignment altogether.

Benjamin was influenced by Surrealist strategies yet took them in a different direction. He brought a historical and redemptive view of liberating the energies contained within detritus, with the aim of de-alienation through the crossing of temporal barriers in the production of constellations between the present and the past (and other times). In this, monadic concentration time is suspended, and the energy contained within commodification is released. This would be the Benjaminian version of heterochronic potential.

Returning to Kitsault and my own attempts to grapple with temporal politics, while my approach is shaped by these ideas, I do not see a direct application of these strategies as particularly viable in this current conjuncture. And regrettably, an eerie methodology of temporal liberation still remains elusive. However, Benjamin's Surrealist influence does provide us with the opening move of, first of all, recognising the everyday present as impenetrable. It is only by acknowledging that the present is as at least somewhat inaccessible that we enter its temporal complexities, yet in everyday life we usually cannot afford this acknowledgement. The modus operandi of the capitalist here and now is to assume it is all self-evident. But with Kitsault there is almost no choice but to admit that the present is lost. It is a training town of the non-present, owing to the fact there is not a lot of here and now present. Its contemporaneity is highly insubstantial—as observed, there is no community life, its economic present is mired in its failed past and in ploys for its future development consisting of extensions of the standard ideas of the present (leisure, resource extraction, wellness commodities, asset value). The social hieroglyphics appear more readily, although their meaning is no less perplexing. Kitsault thrusts the mysterious nature of the present directly at us; and to extrapolate from a 'Kitsault as method' formulation would be to look for Kitsault in logistic sites, in more normal cities or possibly in any quotidian situation.

Kitsault prime

Given how unlikely it is to find a town frozen for 40 years, Kitsault appears like a model rather than an actual place. It is not actual in both senses—not quite real or existing in fact (imaginary despite its material existence), and not active in the present. Kitsault seems like a reconstruction of a time, but not quite like returning to 1980 as if it were a historical village. It has left the usual sequence of years and entered into a suspended realm. And within this condition, it occurs to us that this may have been orchestrated. On any account, we should not think of Kitsault's current state as in any way innocent or accidental. And if it isn't innocent, what is its guilt or knowingness? Not stopping at the short answer (that the mining company closed it due to a fall in price), there is a lot of room for speculation. The paranoid imagination is certainly primed to answer—and the extensive contours of twenty-first-century paranoia are still being defined, accounting for something beyond continual surveillance and auditing within an integration of life into suspicion—with intricate theories as to the sinister purposes, the main players, persecutions, etc. It seems to carry on when the futural imagination falters. But before we can assess the orchestration, as neither a one-line answer nor a delusion and unravel some of the significant dimensions, we realise that the simulated condition triggers vivid perceptions in the way a normal place does not. Even if we found an actual, inhabited town or suburb built at the exact same time, with the same buildings and urban planning (there are plenty of examples to choose from), there would be no astonishment. In fact, there would likely be repulsion. Yet we are pulled into a full immersion with Kitsault. It is enthralling despite its otherwise bland qualities. A complete simulation is engaging in a way an actual town in the here and now would never be, and herein—this rift or lapse, its formation and implications—lies its real fascination.

To use Fisher's term discussed in Chapter 1, Kitsault can be seen as an unworlded ordinary settlement. Unworlding is an event that shatters faith in one's life world. What we held to be real and undeniable now appears as fabricated or a ruse. What was thought to be just life—the sole, self-evident existence—looks as if it is just one version among others, and probably a lesser type. The way Fisher discusses the term gives it a game-like quality, where existence is structured on levels with elevation or relegation driving the players' actions; or the fear that reality is on some other level which one cannot fully access (and one is then marooned on a simulated level); or worse, a realisation that there is no fundamental level at all. Unworlding might have a game-like quality, but it is based on the 'ontological terror. . . —is our own world a simulation?' (Fisher 2016, 47) With Kitsault we can wonder if the town has been moved up or down in ontological significance since its abandonment, or has the game been switched off for almost 40 years? Is the real, master level the commodity market, which allowed Kitsault to be created and then swept it away? Is there a secret hatch in the woods or a door in one of the basements which leads out of here, into rows of flat-screen terminals in an investment office where the whole thing is being controlled, into a logistical absolute space, or into other, still higher levels?

One of the examples Fisher uses to explore the concept is Philip K Dick's fiction which often presents an unworlding that is impending and not yet resolved. 'Some of the most powerful passages in Dick's work are those in which there is an ontological interregnum: a traumatic unworlding is not yet given a narrative motivation; an unresolved space that awaits reincorporation into another symbolic regime' (50). This would seem to be closest to the Kitsault situation. It is not the space of traumatic separation but one of suspended anticipatory time. Consequences are pending, and in the interim, we have been brought into a reality half-light where the town has been stripped away. Like in Dick's *Time Out of Joint*, the protagonists are on a 'passage out of a "realistic" world into an "unworld"' (49). Kitsault has left the naturalist realism of everyday life, like the scenes back in its prime that bloggers and television reports always refer to with families getting ready for school in the morning, sports events in the recreation centre, crowded Friday nights at the Maple Leaf Pub. Bit by bit this realist machinery breaks down leaving a partial or abstracted version of the place which is the Kitsault we encounter now. 'It's a scene in which Edward Hopper seems to devolve into Beckett, as the natural(ist) landscape gives way to an emptied-out monotony, a minimal, quasi-abstract space that is de-peopled but still industrialised and commercialised' (51). The trauma here is anticipatory—pre-traumatic stress.

But Kitsault isn't fiction, and the unworlding here is our own, not limited to the boundaries of this curious site. We do not have such a privileged, spectator position in this unworld. What are called crises—Covid-19, anthropogenic climate change, energy supply disruptions, geopolitical conflicts—are unworlding events or an interval preparing the way. Most of these crises are just a first act lacking full narrative motivation, awaiting a symbolic regime that will assert its world. Given the global scope, it is happening everywhere (unworlding the world); but Kitsault's emptied reality resonates with this unsettling condition. Its miniature unworld can function as a space to come to terms with some elements of this, perhaps to get some purchase before being totally immersed into the world to come.

As the concept of unworlding is built around the fiction of Dick (and also Fassbinder) with its 'is our own world a simulation?' presented within a particular mise-en-scène, it definitely has the mark of the Cold War. The narrative of this unworlding, wherein reality is revealed as a simulation designed to break the mind and extract some bit of information feels like *The Prisoner's* Port Marion or like Vinnytsia, which was an exact copy of a small American town constructed in Ukraine in order to train Soviet spies; or at least, that was the CIA's report (see Bailey 2021). An imaginary town to train real spies. 'A special training facility complete with duplicates of buildings, streets and businesses used to train Soviet agents in Western culture before sending them to the United States.' Vinnytsia (and other such places) seems more like a myth than an actual site, promulgated by American intelligence agencies to instil fear and suspicion in their citizens in the spirit of self-defence and vigilance against an enemy from within. The Soviets had not only rockets and nuclear weapons but also perfect copies of small Midwestern towns where the only genuine feature was the fence surrounding them.

So this version of an unworlded Kitsault has a cold war feel to it, a retro backdrop. It seems ironic that amid the twenty-first century's intense array of simulated realities, this anxiety would feel like it is from the past. Perhaps it is the stage setting of a clearly delineated drama of simulation that is missing from current social life and media environments. It is the relentless applications of simulated spaces and more to the point, melding of actual and simulated, that functions differently than the unworldings of P K Dick. But Kitsault is a training town, after all. Things are laid out in their basic forms. It might be more accurate to label this rendering as an anachronism rather than being merely dated. It is specific to cold wars in general—interregnums between major wars, continual proxy conflicts, counter-insurgency campaigns without end—which seem to have a powerful claim on the future rather than tied to a particular cold war in the second half of the twentieth century.

The more you consider the story that a mining company spent millions on a town that never really existed for more and a year so, the more the doubts creep in. Kitsault was never a mining town. The story of the decline in the molybdenum price was just a cover. Picking such an obscure mineral was a nice touch. So what kind of training was, or should I say, is being conducted here? And why stop at Kitsault—that any town, any section of a city might actually be something other than what it appears. Most 'communities' are not set up primarily to be places of care, to accommodate networks of friends and family, interesting activities, etc. Of course this happens, but underneath are machines for accumulation, the nation state apparatus, and so on. The sleepers have been activated and set about their real tasks.

An alternate to this unworlding drama would be seeing Kitsault as a method stub. The term is from software development referring to a placeholder in programming code that is inserted until a more fully developed version can be produced. It is sometimes used for testing purposes within a larger process of completion. The term has entered broader usage, for example, in the way underdeveloped articles in Wikipedia are referred to as stubs. William Gibson has used it as a trope in the novels *The Peripheral* and *Agency*. In his narratives, which mix virtual and actual worlds freely, stubs are aborted ends of historical development. The novels feature time travel, via a kind of internet linkage, which results in the future meddling into the past and producing offshoots of history that do not lead to the real future. They are branches that lead nowhere, yet their dramas can affect the real course of history, mainly owing to the virtual contract with them. Gibson's *Agency* is disappointing, in that the stubs are seldom very troubling— there is no terror of being unworlded. They are a creative bending of reality to move the plot along, and these partial states are assimilated with relative ease. What would it mean to see Kitsault as a method stub? A future has intervened and killed it off. Within the metaphor of history as software code, with unresolved components, we would then wonder what is the purpose of the overall programme, in what hardware is it situated and who or what directs it? Kitsault would be a placeholder site, which would then be developed at a later date or completely abandoned as seems to be the case. Stubs are probably best applied to thinking of the future as sites of contingency, labour and speculation. How many efforts and projects assume stub forms, and that this whole book can be considered as a method stub—Kitsault's revenge.

Living room with television and chair

A quintessential Kitsault image (appearing on YouTube videos and on websites dedicated to urban exploration or ghost towns) is of a living room in one of the houses. There is a cream coloured carpet and beige walls, electric baseboard heating elements and a large late 1970s wood cabinet television. Beside it is an armchair with a vaguely Scandinavian design made of blond wood with curved arms and dark brown fabric padding. The room is otherwise empty and there is nothing on the walls. The room has a good amount of natural light, and everything looks unused in more or less perfect condition, almost like in a shopping catalogue or travel brochure, except the room is a little too blank and unadorned. There are identical chairs appearing in other photos of Kitsault, such as in the library and other houses. It is a company town after all. On the television screen, switched off, is a reflection of the rest of the room, with a glare of the window. It is uncertain when it was photographed. Presumably, it could have been any time between 1983 and the present. That is the span of its suspension. It took centuries of capitalist modernity—European colonisation, industrial revolutions, the development of vast systems of production and consumption, infrastructures of all kinds, demands for minerals like molybdenum, all the financing and economics of the mining sector, and so much more—for this room to appear as it is. If one had enough resources and cognitive mapping acumen, it would be possible to reverse engineer capitalist modernity from this empty living room frozen for 40 years. But why stop there? With such skill and vision, this living room could be a portal to fabulate other pasts, presents and futures.

Home to Kitsault

With Kitsault, I don't wonder about the classic ghost town fascinations: why did people live here, why did they leave and what did they do while they were here? I know all those answers—they came to mine a minor metal commodity in 1980, they left in 1982 because of a fall in price and the company closed the mine. When they were here they mined and presumably lived in a familiar lifestyle of the time. A year and a half habitation is not long enough to serve as an anchor for all the sufferings and joys of human lives in the way one encounters in tragically abandoned homes or settlements. Kitsault's abandonment is not a scene of a disastrous disintegration of peoples' lives.

In a way it is more comic than tragic. Kitsault is an accidental folly—in the sense of an ostentatious construction with no practical purpose, often a tower or mock-Gothic ruin surrounded by gardens. But here, it is an inert North American subdivision dropped into a northern rain forest. A banal commodity culture monument, without this or that vision of heritage. Its partial preservation is not in the service of an ideology of how the past should be. But it is in this state only by accident, a series of mistakes and coincidences ('down turns' in metal commodity markets, whims of an entrepreneur, tax-write-off scheme, regulatory hold-ups). Kitsault is in a holding pattern, in this sense a lot like many other parts of the world, sections of cities and all the other varieties of Kitsault.

But it *is* a site of calamity and captivation. Yet not in the usual way disaster sites are. Its calamity is extended in a vast chain—disturbed, systemic, it cannot be isolated to particular sites of ruination and instead in the omnipresent calamity of the Anthropocene. Kitsault occurs on a local plane but it is entangled in planetary scales. Ruination haunts most places in one way or another, but this is usually well concealed. But Kitsault is not like another town, it is a joke of a town. And this connects with another standard view of ghost towns in the way they are like movie sets. The ghost town is an arena for our imagination, where we can play a part, wander around the location. Kitsault is an image of frozen squander, and in this, a site of reflection and potentiality. It is—in its suspension—like landing on an area of board game in which a move in any direction can be conceived. And inevitably, a place where comedy turns into tragedy, in the violence of resource extraction, colonial violation, the damaging absurdity of capitalist expenditure and waste—disrupting lives, ecosystems, appropriating vitalities of all kinds on hair-brained schemes and market whims. Kitsault is a place where all of this comes home. The absence of people in this ambiguous setting starts to become unbearable, like a capitalist neutron weapon was tested here eviscerating all the people.

The end of Kitsault (standstills with no time left)

Centuries ago a novel economic system spread around the planet and then altered the climate so that over time viable life became degraded. But captivated in the dream world that makes its denizens oblivious of its end, there's nothing to worry about. We could lie here forever on the sofa in one of these Kitsault living rooms, just looking at the dull reflection of the window on the non-illuminated CRT television screen. Is Kitsault the City of Molybdenum or a failed capitalist Nowa Huta? It would seem at the most to be a waiting room for historical forces to realign. From what kind of future will they arrive? An LNG ship or hydrofoil will appear in the inlet, the artists and doctors will disembark beginning their retreats, the natural gas pipeline finally reaches the coast, the film festival crowds arrive, so too, the barges with garbage for the waste generator station. The realist period-correct answer would be, of course, waiting for the existing infrastructure to break down, waiting for forest fires and floods. Like Lytton BC, not so far away that had several days of temperatures close to 50°C in the summer of 2021 and then burned to the ground, Kitsault could burn. It currently has 200 days of rain per year, but this could change. This is the typical early twenty-first-century expectation of entropy. It's not unreasonable to make Kitsault into an antechamber for the end of the world. But I don't want Kitsault to be a site to place a wager on survival or a 'preppers' paradise. The morbid future of the typically predictive kind—who will survive, what will, what won't. This tendency must be abolished and open to a different kind of thinking and acting.

Most likely its suspended state will soon come to a low-density end. Its owner is aging, facing lawsuits, will he keep putting money into the maintenance? The holding pattern can only be maintained for so long, and his ploys for development have come to nothing. Soon Kitsault will fall away—perhaps after a quick sale or two to other romantic entrepreneurs with visions of artistic retreats or resource extraction—and then finally those frozen constructions will be levelled. If Kitsault disappeared, what precisely would be lost? A portal would close as we move back to the normal outcomes of desertion or redevelopment. A weird gap would be sealed over, and yet, there would still be the countless others that are opening all the time.

Forgetting something that is designed to be forgettable within the wrong kind of impermanence. Somethings just weren't meant to last. Like remembering every coke can you have ever handled. Kitsault is a miniscule moment. It is not bound in amnesia but incapable of a history and a future. We assume it will always be the same, each time it is thrown away. We assume some inertia will always animate things. This juvenile aspect of capitalist time. It is going to be ok—you'll have your treats, your unboxing, holidays, fancy meals, it will go on as always. Those with vast wealth, the rich people in the cemeteries and their children, they've made future arrangements.

How much time is left? Losing time, valuable time which cannot be restored. Is all of this just playing with time, as if we have all the time in the world? Standstills are not a fantasy of stopping time. What is required is the suspension of business-as-usual—the material form of contemporary capitalism (Malm 2021, 37). Suspension in the time of accelerated climate change is exactly what is required—urgency *and* pause.

There's nothing to wait for here, and nothing will ever arrive in Kitsault. If we are waiting for anything, it is for us to release our own time under these unique conditions, into a variety of forms and speculative modes. This has already begun. Suthanthiran's idea that Kitsault could become a kind of brain camp for thinking through the world's major problems could only be realised through its abandonment and resulting atmosphere. It can now become a world centre of dialectics at a standstill and eerie cognitive mapping. Kitsault's present is most of all one of strange fascination—video podcasts, news reports, ghost town tours and academic reflections on temporal politics. In the end, that is its most successful role. I don't think it will ever be anything else. Its owner will die and the media interest will fade, and we will have lost Kitsault as a space but not as an enigma.

Note

1 'It is easier to imagine the end of the world than the end of capitalism' is an endlessly referenced statement attributed to Jameson (although there is no published text where he directly states it) and Žižek (who makes this declaration yet posits it as coming from Jameson). For Fisher, it encapsulates capitalist realism in 'the widespread sense that not only is capitalism the only viable political and economic system, but also that it is now impossible even to imagine a coherent alternative to it' (Fisher 2009, 2). This slogan has entered a long and intense half-life phase, and part of its decay is its own self-fulfilling prophecy. The crux of the phrase really lies in the status of imaginative capacities or lack thereof. How the words 'end,' 'world' and 'capitalism' are understood is an expression of these imaginative energies or their impoverishment.

References

Bailey, Travis Lee. 2021. '1960 Soviet Spy School spy town CIA Educational Documentary Vinnytsia Ukraine.' [YouTube Video]. Accessed August 23, 2021.

Barton, Jason. 2017. 'On Vanishing Land.' Interview by Robin MacKay. In *The Fisher-Function*, edited by Lendl Barcelos, Matt Colquhoun, Ashiya Eastwood, Kodwo Eshun, Moalemi Mahan and Geelia Ronkina, 73–118. London: Egress.

Benjamin, Walter. 1999a. *The Arcades Project*. Cambridge, MA: Belknap Press of Harvard University Press.

Benjamin, Walter. 1999b. *Selected Writings, Vol 2*. Cambridge, MA: Harvard University Press.

CBC/Radio Canada. 'B.C. Ghost Town Could Become Major Natural Gas Hub.' *CBC News*. CBC/Radio Canada, July 31 2013. Accessed May 23, 2020. www.cbc.ca/news/canada/british-columbia/b-c-ghost-town-could-become-major-natural-gas-hub-1.1391052

Chukhrov, Keti. 2020. *Practicing the Good: Desire and Boredom in Soviet Socialism*. Minneapolis: University of Minnesota Press.

Coolidge, Carrie. 2008. 'Ghosts for Sale.' *Forbes* 182 (2) (August 11): 104.

Danowski, Dborah. and Viveiros de Castro, Eduardo. 2017. *The Ends of the World*. Malden, MA: Polity.

Dembicki, Geoff. 2013. 'David Black's Refinery Wild Card Gets Wilder.' *The Tyee. ca*, May 7, 2013.

Fisher, Mark. 2009. *Capitalist Realism*. Winchester: Zero Books.

Fisher, Mark. 2016. *The Weird and Eerie*. London: Repeater Books.

Jameson, Fredric. 2020. *The Benjamin Files*. London: Verso Books.

Kitsault Resorts. 'About Kitsault.' Kitsault. Kitsault Resorts, n.d. Accessed June 12, 2020. www.kitsault.com/about_hist.html

Malm, Andreas. 2021. *How to Blow Up a Pipeline*. London: Verso.

Osborne, Peter. 1995. *The Politics of Time*. London: Verso.

Rosa, Hartmut. 2013. *Social Acceleration*. New York: Columbia University Press.

Struck, Doug. 2005. 'Virginia Millionaire Buys Himself a Ghost Town.' *Washington Post Saturday,* July 30, 2005.

Index

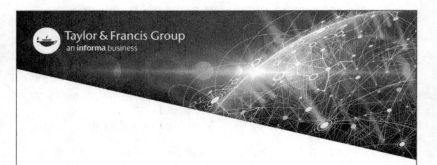

Printed in the United States
by Baker & Taylor Publisher Services